KEEPING
LITTLE
BLIGHTERS
BUSY

CLAIRE POTTER

Illustrated by • MARK BEECH

To my own adorable little blighters,
big Fred and little Lola

Published 2012 by Featherstone Education
Bloomsbury Publishing Plc
50 Bedford Square, London,
www.acblack.com

ISBN 978-1-4081-7624-5

Text © Claire Potter 2012
Ilustrations © Mark Beech 2012

Printed in Great Britain by Martins The Printers, Berwick-upon-Tweed

1 3 5 7 9 10 8 6 4 2

This book is produced using paper that is made from wood grown in
managed, sustainable forests. It is natural, renewable and recyclable.
The logging and manufacturing processes conform to the environmental
regulations of the country of origin.

To see our full range of titles visit www.acblack.com

CONTENTS

DESIGN AND CONSTRUCTION

Inventive projects for designing and making in a 'real life' way

CHINWAGGERS

Unique and stimulating ideas to really get them talking

WORDSMITHS

Original and creative ways to experiment with the written word

HIDDEN TREASURE

Two ingenious treasure hunts, one for big kids and one for little ones

SPICING UP EVERYDAY LIFE 92

Add an element of surprise and fun to the day-to-day routine

GARDEN ANTICS 106

Imaginative ideas to keep them entertained and happy in your own back garden

'TIS THE SEASON TO BE... 116

Fresh inspiration to help celebrate those special days of the year

INTRODUCTION

From the moment my son was born, he was feisty, alert, ready to explore and seemed to want more from the world than milk and cuddles! By the age of one, if I hadn't taken him out by mid morning, he was banging on the front door. When I took him to toddler groups, instead of playing with the toys, he'd circle the edges of the room, looking for ways out, exploring corridors, stairs, fire escapes. I found myself taking him for walks in thunderstorms or – if I just couldn't face the rain – building him assault courses with furniture in the living room! Crikey, I thought, this parenting thing is really hard.

Yet, it forced me early on to think creatively and alternatively about how to keep him entertained – without constantly spending money. I thought back to my own childhood and tuned into that playful, adventurous, slightly mischievous way of approaching the world which led to all sorts of antics with my sister and friends...like wading along a stream to see how far we could follow it out of town...or dressing up very convincingly as an old lady and walking past my mum in the street! Walking, shopping, eating, having a bath... All it needed was a twist and a tweak, a touch of boldness and some upside-down thinking.

When we adopted my daughter seven years later, she was a breeze. Calm, home loving, self-contained and endlessly creative. Give her a piece of corrugated cardboard and a hole punch and one hour later she'd have created her own lift-the-flap book! This led to thinking up all sorts of quirky things we could do without even stepping out the door. If we were going to do art, we could do better than a colouring book. If we were going to do cooking, we could go beyond a batch of fairy cakes. (I wanted things which appealed to me too!)

These days there are so many ready-made attractions we can take our children to, and so much 'stuff' we can buy them, but creating our own fun from scratch can be much more fulfilling. Research shows that good and memorable experiences increase our happiness level far more than any possession ever will. Think back to your own childhood and I bet the biggest, warmest, fuzziest feelings come from things you did rather than things you got. Just present an activity to your children with a bit of pizzazz – or as a surprise – to psyche them up for it and off you go...

Wishing you lots of mini-adventures and out-of-the-ordinary fun!

Claire Potter

FOOD DUDES

Exciting challenges and alternative ways to experience food

- Supermarket Challenge
- Lickety Wallpaper
- Lucky Dip Cooking
- It's Gone all Mouldy!
- The Dinner Party Experiment BRAVE + BOLD!
- The Day of the Chopsticks

Supermarket Challenge

Are your kids fed up with being dragged around the supermarket? Why not make it a race against time and a test of their resourcefulness!

What you need:

- A supermarket
- A fiver

A bit of background

When kids hit around 6 or 7, the supermarket suddenly becomes the most boring place in the world. They thought it was such fun when they were toddlers, sticking price labels on the fruit and vegetables, gawping at the fish on the fish counter and 'helping' to put items in the trolley. Now it's just moan, groan, and can't-we-go-home!

I was in this particular situation one day. Heading home from the park with my (then) 8-year-old son and his friend, I remembered we had no food in the cupboard. We needed at the very least something to eat for dinner that evening. The boys dragged and scuffed their feet in protest. I was about as enthusiastic as them but there was no choice.

Then, a brainwave! Let *them* buy dinner and turn it into a game. And so was born the 'Supermarket Challenge'.

What we did

I gave them £5 and 15 minutes to choose and buy dinner, which I would cook. As I didn't fancy eating chicken nuggets and curly fries, I made three rules:

> Rule 1. No convenience foods – they must buy ingredients to cook from scratch with.
> Rule 2. There must be some vegetables or salad.
> Rule 3. There must be at least two courses.

They were off in a cloud of dried mud.

Meanwhile, I sat in the supermarket café with my toddler and a cup of tea, occasionally catching a glimpse of them dashing down an aisle or stopping to do some maths on their fingers. I was very curious to see what they would buy – and a little bit apprehensive!

The result ☆

13½ minutes later and 5p under budget, I met them at the checkout and was astonished by what they had managed to get – a four-course meal!

TIP: Prime your children first with some useful tactics such as getting more for their money with basics/value or reduced price products. Saving time by asking staff where items are located.

Course 1: Carton of pea and ham soup

Course 2: Corn on the cob

Course 3: Ingredients for spaghetti bolognaise

Course 4: Lemon meringue pie

'Next time,' my son said, 'I want 4 pounds and 10 minutes!'

Okay, so it was a bit short on the vegetables and courses 1 and 4 were a little on the 'ready' side – and I'm not quite sure why they got potatoes to go with spaghetti bolognaise – but overall I was impressed.

They were rather pleased with themselves too and tucked into their meal with more relish than usual that evening. We were all stuffed by the end of it.

☞ IF YOU LIKE THIS, YOU MIGHT LIKE SHOPKEEPERS' TREASURE HUNT P.000

Lickety Wallpaper

Make lickable wallpaper for your kids lickety-split* – the easy way! (*lickety-split *adverb* very fast, with great speed)

What you need:

- A computer and printer
- Gloss photo paper
- A saucepan
- Boiled sweets (different colours and flavours)
- A paintbrush

Age: 3–10

A bit of background

What child can resist the idea of lickable wallpaper? It totally captures the inventive, sensual, playful spirit of *Willy Wonka and the Chocolate Factory*. Well here's an incredibly quick and easy way to make it for your children without any of the complicated or high-tech cooking processes that you might find in other recipes. The result is every bit as effective and delicious!

What I did

I bought some bags of boiled sweets of different colours. Where possible, I got ones with fruit flavours – strawberry, apple, lemon, orange and blackcurrant – but I didn't worry too much about this. The only red ones I could find, for example, were mixed berry flavour and the green ones just seemed to be 'green' flavour!

Then I found individual pictures of each type of fruit on the Internet by

Googling 'Strawberry', 'Apple' and so on, in images. I went for illustrations rather than photos as I thought they'd look more 'wallpaperish'. (It doesn't really matter what size the images are – mine were roughly 4 x 4 cm.)

Using the computer, I pasted the images into a document in vertical lines so that there was a strawberry, an apple, a lemon, an orange and a bunch of blackcurrants in each line. (I managed to get three lines on one page.) Then I printed them out onto glossy, white, A4 photo paper which was robust enough to take the flavouring without disintegrating. Next I cut the paper into separate strips.

To make the flavouring, I melted the boiled sweets in a pan – one colour at a time – over a very low heat until they were a thick, gooey consistency. Then I used a small paintbrush to paint the goo onto the strips of paper on the appropriate fruit: red on the strawberry, green on the apple and so on. (Leave the pan on a low heat while you are doing this or the sweets will go hard again.) You don't need to be particularly neat or careful as long as there's a good spread of flavour on each fruit – but you do need to be quite quick because the liquid solidifies almost immediately.

NB: The melted sweets are extremely hot so keep children away from this bit!

Then I stuck the 'wallpaper strips' up at lickable height and let the kids at them! It's best to assign one strip to each child to prevent it becoming a germ-swapping fest!

The result ☆

My daughter and her friends were thrilled with it. And it really is the funniest sight to see children with their little, pointy pink tongues sticking out, licking the wall furiously and laughing!

 TIP: Lickable wallpaper is great for kids' parties! Put a strip on the wall for each guest – or give them each a strip to take home in their party bag.

 AND ANOTHER IDEA...
The Taste Test: Prepare lots of tiny tasters of food e.g. Marmite, a morsel of carrot, peanut butter, a cornflake, a frozen pea... Blindfold your children and pop the food into their mouths one by one. Can they guess what each one is? Don't tell them until the end how many they got right.

 IF YOU LIKE THIS, YOU MIGHT LIKE... JAM TART TRAY DINNER P.94

Lucky Dip Cooking

If someone gave you a random bag of ingredients, could you make something delicious?

What you need:

- A bag of ingredients to make a meal

Age: 5 to grown-up

A bit of background

This idea was inspired by the TV programme *Ready Steady Cook!* Celebrity chefs are given a bag of food bought by someone else (with a price limit) and challenged to knock up a tasty meal in 20 minutes.

Catching a bit of that programme one afternoon, my son (then 12) said, 'Hey, we could actually do that you know.' So that weekend we did – adapting it slightly to suit non-professional child cooks! These were our rules:

THE RULES:

Rule 1. A £6 price limit on the bag of food.

Rule 2. No time limit. (We're not used to cooking under time pressure. If we didn't finish cooking our meal, it would be a waste of food and we'd have nothing to eat!)

Rule 3. We agreed that we wouldn't deliberately make the mix of ingredients too bizarre and difficult to cook with. (But we might make it a little adventurous or throw in a red herring!)

Rule 4. Access to any basic 'larder' ingredients we wanted e.g. onions, stock, butter, milk, flour, tomato puree, spices, etc.

What we did

We decided, as my daughter was only 6, our teams would be boys (dad and son) versus girls (mum and daughter), but if your children are older and reasonably competent cooks, you could do kid versus kid or adults versus kids. The randomness of the ingredients makes it more of a level playing field.

Boys were to go first. Girls would follow the next weekend. So my daughter and I set off to the supermarket. I wanted to give her the dominant role in choosing the ingredients but I knew it would be tricky for a young child so I helped her by getting her to choose a protein, a carbohydrate, a vegetable and so on (she'd recently learnt these terms in school!). It was quite a challenge to stay inside our price limit — there was lots of weighing and pricing of vegetables and some painful mental arithmetic — but that added to the fun!

In the end, we chose:
Red lentils, goat's cheese, beetroot, coriander, and orange pepper

When we got home, the 'boys' delved into their bag with curiosity and were both pleased and flummoxed! The level of challenge was just about right — neither of them had cooked with lentils before for a start. We left them to it in the kitchen and 45 minutes later, dinner was served!

Starter
Slices of goat's cheese and beetroot in a balsamic dressing (presented in a very elegant Mastercheffy fashion by my son)
Main course: Lentil, pepper and coriander soup with croutons (and bread from the larder)

The result ☆

It was genuinely very tasty. My son had learnt to make dressing and soup – two things he'd never done before. It had also pushed inventiveness – we had never eaten or expected to eat those exact dishes in our house. No pressure for the girls then!

TIP: Give young children a sweet rather than a savoury bag of ingredients. Puddings are easier to make because they're more about presentation and less about cooking skills. Any sweet ingredients put together somehow are likely to taste pretty good!

 IF YOU LIKE THIS, YOU MIGHT LIKE...THE LEFT-RIGHT WALK P.24

It's Gone All Mouldy!

Grow a fungus farm. It'll fascinate the kids – in a repulsive kind of way!

What you need:

- Jars with lids (or cling film)
- Card or stickers for labels
- A pen
- Pieces of food from your fridge and cupboards

Age: 3–10

A bit of background

When I was a kid, I remember discovering a forgotten bowl of cornflakes under my friend's bed, completely covered in green splodges of furry mould. Although it was utterly disgusting, I was intrigued by it and couldn't help staring, examining the shapes, the colours and the general 'urrghhhnesss'.

Children are fascinated by anything gross, disgusting and repulsive. Look at the success of *Horrible Histories* for example. Now I would do anything to get rid of the ugly mildew in my bathroom but I thought, I bet it would be really interesting for the kids if we did the very opposite and actually encouraged mould to grow.

What we did

We collected old jars (jam, peanut butter, olives, etc.) and gave them a good wash. Any number of jars, between say five and ten, would do.

We put a piece of damp tissue at the bottom of each one to make a nice, moist, mould-friendly environment! Then into each jar we put a different piece of food. You could use any foods, but good ones to use are:

cheese, bread, carrot, apple, orange, bacon, onion

Next, we put the lids on the jars and made a few small air holes in them. You could cover the jars with cling film instead and make air holes in that. Then, for that 'museumy' feel – and because the food might eventually become unrecognisable – we made labels out of small pieces of folded card placed in front of each jar (stickers on the lid would do too).

All that was left to do was line the jars up in a warm, sunny place like on the window sill (or near a radiator in the winter) and then…well, wait.

The result ☆

It took a little patience but after about a week the first splodge of fungus appeared (different foods will grow mould at different rates). And then it grew and festered and multiplied until we had an astonishing array of gruesome moulds – there was bright green, furry, white, round, grey, irregular, black dots, blotchy – like a catalogue of horrible plague-like diseases from medieval times.

The kids loved it! Each morning they came downstairs eagerly to examine the progress and pull faces of disgust and pleasure. They also thoroughly enjoyed showing their fungus farm to visitors to gross them out.

You could make a chart for them to record their observations – how many days it took for the mould to appear on each food, the speed of growth, the colour, the shape etc.

You could even let them take photos of the progression like an investigator at a crime scene!

Leave the fungus farm for as long as you can bear it! (Ours was on our mantelpiece for several months.)

 BEWARE! Make absolutely sure that your kids know not to touch – or eat! – the fungus. Keep the jars covered at all times. You don't want allergic reactions or food poisoning!

 TIP: Have a magnifying glass handy to get a really good look at that nasty fungus!

 IF YOU LIKE THIS, YOU MIGHT LIKE...BUTTERFLY COLLECTOR P.44

The Dinner Party Experiment

It's a bit scary and a bit risky – but letting your child host a dinner party all by themselves has more benefits than downsides!

BRAVE + BOLD!

What you need:

- Dinner party ingredients
- Willing guests

Age: 10 upwards

A bit of background

One day, when my son was 11, he suddenly announced that he wanted to host a dinner party – for adults – and do *all* the planning, cooking and serving himself! My immediate reaction was eek-squirm-umm-oh-but-you-only-know-how-to-make-beans-on-toast-and-pasta-with-pesto! But I didn't want to crush his enthusiasm and confidence (over-ambition?) so I bit my tongue and said something like, 'Mmm, that's a good idea...let me have a think about how that could work!'

I decided that if he learnt and practised the dishes first until I was satisfied that he could be left alone in the kitchen to get on with it *and* the food would taste reasonably good, it could be fun and esteem-building for him – plus we'd get to relax and socialize while he did all the work!

What we did

We looked through recipe books together and he chose three relatively easy but dinner-party-worthy courses:

Carrot and coriander soup

Pasta with a pork and rosemary sauce

Butterscotch bread and butter pudding

18

The beauty was that only the pasta would actually need to be cooked 'live' on the night. Everything else could be prepared during the day and then heated on the hob or cooked in the oven before serving.

First he practised cooking the dishes with me – although I tried to 'direct' rather than help him too much. A week or two later, he cooked them again for our family dinner. Next we needed to find some laid-back and forgiving friends to be the guinea pigs (I mean guests!) for his dinner party. We found a willing couple and a date was set.

On the big day, he spent the afternoon cooking as well as making name place cards and a menu (his idea). He set the table with candles and also – for laughs – decided to wear a shirt and bow tie (found in the dressing-up box).

The result ☆

The evening went really well and we were proud. The food was good (I could pick holes – over al dente pasta, pudding burnt slightly round the edges...but I won't!). I also managed to resist the temptation to take control and keep popping in the kitchen.

TIP:
• If you choose dishes that can be completely or mostly prepared in advance, it takes the pressure off on the night!

• A younger sibling could be a waiter and assistant to the Head Chef!

AND ANOTHER IDEA...

Blackboard Placemats:
Teach very young children how to lay the table – and make it a chore they want to do! Get some cheap vinyl or wooden placemats, sand them a little and then paint them with blackboard paint. Use chalk to draw the shape of a plate, knife, fork, spoon and a circle for the cup or glass to show them where everything goes. They can use the placemats to draw and doodle on before and after mealtimes.

IF YOU LIKE THIS, YOU MIGHT LIKE... JAM TART TRAY DINNER P.94

The Day of the Chopsticks

Kids love the idea of using chopsticks – and this four-level challenge will make getting to grips with them more pleasurable than painful!

What you need:

- Wooden tong chopsticks (easy to get from chain sushi or noodle bars)
- Ordinary chopsticks
- Elastic bands,
- Small pieces of paper
- Jam tart/muffin trays
- Bowls
- Sweets of different sizes

A bit of background

When children see a pair of chopsticks for the first time, they are always curious and enthusiastic. 'How do you use these?' they say, picking them up and experimenting. Usually, they give up pretty quickly when they realise it's not something they can learn instantly – or they sense from the grown-ups that it's too tricky for kids. But in China and Japan, you see children as young as 2 or 3 shoveling slippery noodles into their mouths with chopsticks. So there is no physiological reason why our children can't learn to use chopsticks from a similar age. They aren't *really* harder to eat with than a knife and fork – they just use different muscles.

So, how about going with their natural curiosity and enthusiasm and psyching them up to conquer chopsticks in a day!

What we did

I chose a weekend day and set my children this challenge with four levels. (If you can't use chopsticks yourself, you could do it too!)

Level 1: *Eat breakfast with a pair of children's chopsticks*
These are like a small pair of wooden tongs – or a giant pair of tweezers! Sushi bars or chain noodle bars are usually happy to give you a handful of them whether you eat there or not. Most cereals (other than porridge!) are easy to eat with these. Cut toast into small squares so they can eat that with chopsticks too. Now your children are used to the idea of using 'sticks' to eat with.

Level 2: *Eat lunch with real chopsticks – joined together with an elastic band!* The elastic band is the equivalent of stabilisers on a bike! Wrap an elastic band reasonably tightly about an inch from the thick ends of the chopsticks (flat disposable chopsticks are less slippery to use than the smooth, rounded, non-disposable ones). Then put a little wedge of folded paper between the chopsticks just below the elastic band. Eating with these requires more concentration and you naturally hold these more like you would hold normal chopsticks.

Level 3: *Pick up and move sweets with ordinary chopsticks* – you can only eat the ones you manage to move! Prepare a jam tart/muffin tray for each child with a few sweets of different types and sizes in each hollow e.g. marshmallows (easy to pick up), wine gums (easyish), bonbons (not too bad), chocolate buttons (quite hard), tic tacs (really hard!). Show your children how to hold and use ordinary chopsticks (see diagram). Their challenge is to transfer the sweets from the tray to a bowl placed at the other end of the room, starting with the largest sweets and working down to the smallest!

Level 4: Now the biggy – eat dinner with ordinary chopsticks! Knives, forks and spoons are strictly banned, but food in a bowl is easier than food on a plate.

 TIP: Perservere! Motivate! No pain, no gain! Think of the sense of achievement they will feel when they've learned to use chopsticks. And it's a skill for life!

How to hold chopsticks

Rest the thick end of one chopstick in the crook of your thumb and forefinger. Rest the lower part lightly against your ring and little finger.

Hold the other chopstick between the tips of your middle and index fingers. Anchor it with your thumb like you would hold a pencil.

Now move the top chopstick up and down and keep the other one still.

TIP: Mothers in China often use this image: Imagine the chopsticks are the beak of a hungry baby bird! When it opens and closes it to ask for food, only the top beak moves.

 IF YOU LIKE THIS, YOU MIGHT LIKE...THE MUSIC TREE P.108

WALK THIS WAY!

Turn a walk into an adventure with these out-of-the-ordinary ideas

- The Left-right Walk
- The Straight Line Walk
- Don't Forget to Smell the Flowers BRAVE + BOLD!
- The Dice-throwing Walk
- Hansel and Gretel Walk
- Time Travel

The Left-right Walk

Turn left. Turn right. It sounds simplistic but it'll put a spring in the step of your children!

Age: 3–13

What you need:

- **Nothing** – except legs and energy!

A bit of background

Sometimes I just want to go for a family walk – fresh air, exercise and a bit of sunlight if I'm lucky! My kids, however, don't generally share my enthusiasm – they'd rather stay at home, stare at a wall and develop rickets than take me up on such a ridiculous suggestion!

However, I found a simple way to trick them into actually *wanting* to go for a walk! The secret is to turn the walk into a kind of game. This distracts them from the fact that they are putting one foot in front of the other. Here's how.

What you do

Tell your children you are going on a 'left-right walk'. You will begin your walk by taking the first left turning, then the next right turning, then the next left turning and so on: Left, right, left, right, left, right (without any control over where you are going or where you will end up).

You could begin at your own front door and find yourself discovering streets and alleyways in your own neighbourhood that you'd never seen before. Or you could drive to somewhere particular (urban or rural) that you'd like to explore.

Let your children be the leaders, in charge of telling you when to turn left and when to turn right. If you come to a dead end, turn back, and take the next left (if you turned left last time) or the next right (if you turned right last time). Then continue alternating as before.

You can end the walk after a time limit that you pre-set yourselves, when you're tired or when you come across somewhere that feels like a natural full-stop – like a cafe, play park or ice-cream shop! We found that this walk tends to take you roughly in a circle anyway and you often end up not too far from where you started!

SAME BUT DIFFERENT: **The Coin Walk**:
Take a coin with you and throw it every time you come to a junction. If it lands on heads, go left. If it lands on tails, go right (if there's no left turn or right turn, continue straight on).

TIP: This walk works best where there are definite paths to follow such as in a town, a woods or a residential area – rather than just open countryside!

IF YOU LIKE THIS, YOU MIGHT LIKE.... THE STRAIGHT LINE WALK P.26

The Straight Line Walk

Draw a line randomly on a map – and then see if you can follow it!

(or whenever your child can walk reasonable distances)

What you need:

- A map of your local area
- A pen

A bit of background

During one school summer holiday day in the '70s, when my sister and I were about 12 and 9, we wanted to go to the town centre. But to spice it up, we decided we'd walk there in a straight line, as the crow flies – or as near a straight line as we could manage. It was really exciting, climbing over walls and wiggling our way round alleys and through bits of rough ground we hadn't noticed before. Being in a particularly devil-may-care mood, we actually took it a bit too far, dashing through someone's open house (we could see they had both their front and back door open) and jumping over a wall to land in some wet concrete. (I wonder if those footprints are still there today!).

What we did

Now, as a responsible parent, I have tried the straight line walk again with my children – without any trespassing or monkey business this time! I got my son to randomly draw a long, straight line on a map of our nearest city from one edge of the page to another in any direction. The line happened to go across an area of the city that was entirely new to us. We chose a good starting point on the line, drove to that spot and parked. Map in hand, our aim was to follow the line on foot as closely as possible.

It was much more fun than an ordinary walk. Suddenly the children were curious and excited about what was round every corner. It made them notice more, think harder, feel adventurous. We came across some very wacky houses, found a rugby ball in the bushes, saw and talked to some children selling their old toys outside their house, discovered a brightly coloured gravestone made out of a rudder near the houseboats... We kept going along the line until we felt it was the right time to stop and then caught a bus back to our starting point.

The result ☆

The children walked much further than they would normally want to. Easily tricked!

 TIP: A pedometer can really encourage a child to walk further. They'll love knowing how many miles they've done.

 SAME BUT DIFFERENT: **The shape walk**: Instead of a straight line, you could draw a shape on the map: A circle, a square, a triangle...

 IF YOU LIKE THIS, YOU MIGHT LIKE...SECRET CHRISTMAS MISSION P.120

Don't Forget to Smell the Flowers!

See familiar streets with fresh eyes – and get others to do the same

What you need:

- Balsa wood pieces (about 10 x 10cm is a good size)
- Waterproof tape
- Felt-tip pens

A bit of background

'*There aren't many people in this world who really know how to look. Usually one glance is enough to register that the grass is green and the sky is blue ...I want you to start noticing things. Once you get used to doing it you'll never be able to stop. It's the best game in the world.*'

This quote, from the children's book *The Last of the Really Great Whangdoodles* by Julie Andrews Edwards, got me thinking. Wherever you happen to live, there are streets you walk down over and over again – the route to school, the way to the corner shop, the walk to the park. You're so used to them that you walk on autopilot and go from A to B barely looking. There's nothing new or interesting to see. Nothing to remark on.

Or is there?

What we did

One Sunday afternoon in autumn, I told my almost 6-year-old daughter we were going for a walk. It sounded uninspiring: We were going to start at our house and walk down ordinary roads, roads that we'd walked down hundreds of times before. BUT, I said, this time we were going to switch on all our senses FULL BLAST so that we noticed small details that we'd never noticed before. They might be beautiful things such as the vibrant colour of a flower or Autumn leaf, interesting things such as something in someone's window or unusual, surprising things. We were going to write and put a notice on or by each thing to alert others walking down the same roads – and make their walk more enjoyable.

She was up for it. We took a pile of small balsa wood pieces (heavier and more noticeable than paper), some waterproof tape (in case we needed to stick the sign to something), and a pack of different colour felt-tip pens. And off we went.

Two minutes down the road, my daughter complained, 'But there's nothing special here.' 'That's because you're so used to this road,' I said, 'So you're not really looking... look up there.' I pointed to some grapes growing by someone's front wall. 'I bet not many people notice them.'

Suddenly she gets it. 'Look at those flowers. They're a really nice colour,' she says, pointing to some purple and yellow pansies growing around a small war memorial. Then she surprises me. 'Let's smell them.' She leans over to smell one and announces it has a strong smell – like honey. I smell too. It's true. 'Let's write a notice,' she says. 'Write: STOP! *Smell these flowers. They smell exactly like honey. Really!*'

From then on there's no stopping her. Here are some of the other notices she placed:

STOP! *Look at this cracked window – what does it remind you of? (It's in the shape of a spider's web)*

LOOK! *How many names can you find in this graffiti? We found 21! (At a bus shelter)*

TOUCH! *See how sharp the leaves of this holly tree are!*

STOP! SNIFF THE AIR! *Can you smell the beer being made at the brewery?*

LOOK UP! *What do you see? (A huge Buddha and a toy giraffe in a high, jutting-out window of an apartment)*

The result ☆

An hour-and-a-bit, two miles, and 22 notices later, we're back home. We've had fresh air, exercise, fun and a valuable lesson in opening our eyes. We even (strangely enough) found a photo of a friend on the ground. Would we have found that if we hadn't switched on our senses?

 IF YOU LIKE THIS, YOU MIGHT ALSO LIKE PIN-IN-THE-MAP SKETCHING P.42

The Dice-throwing Walk

A simple little dice can add a big element of fun and randomness to a family walk

What you need:

- A dice
- A pen
- A piece of paper

A bit of background

Here's how to turn an ordinary walk into an exciting game of chance and discovery – and change a reluctant trudge into a lively escapade! All you need is a dice and some willing volunteers!

What you do

Tell your children that you are going to leave it entirely in the hands of fate to decide the route of your walk – by throwing a dice! The dots on the dice are a special code in which each number from 1 to 6 stands for a different instruction, like this:

Write this code down on a piece of paper and take it with you on your walk, along with the dice. Choose an area for your walk which has definite paths rather than just open

1: Go straight on.

2: Go left.

3: Go right.

4: Child can choose which way you go.

5: Parent can choose which way you go.

6: Turn back on yourselves.

countryside – for example, an urban area or woods with lots of tracks in it. You could even use the dice for a walk round the block.

Now every time you come to any sort of junction on your walk and have a choice of which way to go, let the children throw the dice (they can take it in turns.) See what number lands face up, consult the code and do what it says! If, on occasions, it tells you to do something that's just not possible – like go left/right/straight on when there isn't that option – simply throw the dice again for a different instruction.

After we got back from our first dice-throwing walk, my daughter immediately set about inventing new instructions for the dice which we could use on other walks!

 TIP: Make sure your children throw the dice gently on the ground just in front of themselves – otherwise you could lose it in the bushes or down a drain! It's probably best to take a spare one just in case!

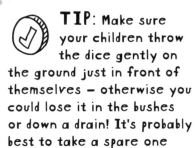 **SAME BUT DIFFERENT**:

Code making: Let your children have fun inventing their own codes for the dice and then try them out. The possibilities are endless: Go in the direction with the narrowest/widest path; go in the direction that you can see an animal (bird, cow, dog being walked...); go in the direction that one of you points to after they've been spun round with their eyes closed!

 IF YOU LIKE THIS, YOU MIGHT LIKE BLACK-OUT POEMS P.84

The Hansel and Gretel Walk

A walk in the woods becomes much more enticing when there's a trail to make and follow

What you need:

- A wood to walk in

A bit of background

We were walking in a woods one day when my daughter said, 'What if we get lost in here?... I know, we could leave a trail of pebbles like Hansel and Gretel.' It instantly took me back to happy memories of my childhood when my sister, cousins and I would spend hours in the woods – in the days when kids were allowed to roam freely – setting up trails for each other to follow using arrows made out of twigs. I wondered if I was remembering it through rose-tinted spectacles, but when we tried it with big (two 13-year-olds) and small (two 6-year-old) kids – they loved it too.

What we did

We went to a wood with a delicious choice of paths and tracks and split into two teams, with an adult in each (you don't want to leave any children on their own!). One team – the 'twiggers' – set off into the woods in advance of the others, collecting twigs from the forest floor and using them to make arrows to show the route they were taking.

The most important thing was to place a clear arrow at every junction to show which way they'd chosen (even if they chose straight on!), but it was also good to have the occasional reassuring arrow in between junctions. The arrows needed to be very obviously 'hand-made' so that they stood out from all the other twigs and debris underfoot. The best way to do this is by using extra large sticks to make the arrows, or piling small twigs on top of each other.

The other team – the 'twoggers' – then set off about 15-20 minutes later. I let the children get all the pleasure and satisfaction of spotting the arrows first (not letting on when I'd already seen one). It really was quite exciting discovering them – for the children and the adults! Eventually, we came to a clearing and saw 'THE END' written with twigs – and the other team hiding behind a tree! Even the younger children were disappointed that the trail was over – and they'd been walking for about an hour. (You can decide a rough time limit before you set off.) The twoggers, all pink cheeks and smiles, were very pleased with themselves too for leading us through the woods so successfully.

✓ TIPS:

• Leave at least a 15 minute gap between the teams setting off – otherwise the twoggers may be able to see the twiggers ahead of them – which will spoil the fun.

• It's a good idea to try to end the trail not too far from where you started – but if the twiggers retrace their steps at any point, they must get rid of any arrows they made earlier that are pointing in the wrong direction!

• Take mobile phones with you, just in case you lose the trail!

IF YOU LIKE THIS, YOU MIGHT LIKE...LUCKY DIP COOKING P.14

Time Travel

Go on a walk around your town or city and travel back 100 years!

What you need:

- Some historical books of your area with lots of photos

A bit of background

On our hallway wall, there's a photo from the 1920s of the road we live in. Stopping to look at it one day, my son started examining exactly how it had changed since then: The road was wider, the pub's sign had changed, Dix's the bakers was just an ordinary house now, children didn't play in the middle of the road anymore... Watching him playing this sort of 'then and now' spot the difference game, I realized we could take it one step further.

What we did

I went to the library and got a whole bunch of local history books full of photos of our town dating back to about 1900. Flicking through them, I chose five or six locations in the town which had an interesting selection of photos and planned a route around the town from one to the other: The Green in the centre of town, the High Street, a spot by the river... Right, I told the kids, we are going on a 'time travel' walk, back to the old days.

When we got to each point, we sat down and scrutinised the old photos and compared them to the place as it was now. I asked them to pinpoint exactly where we were in the photos and pick out as many changes as they could. There were so many details to pick up on: different lampposts, different shops, lack of TV aerials...

The photos of The Green, for example, showed sheep grazing all over it as it was common land then, and farmers' wives selling dairy products underneath a stone structure called the Buttercross ('You only get teenagers hanging out there now!' said my son). He was particularly interested in a photo that showed two houses that had been bombed in the war. He went into detective mode and found two dents in the building where shrapnel had hit the walls and a piece of missing kerbside.

My daughter liked the human elements best. Down by the river, we looked at a photo of two women punting in frilly shirts and long skirts, and another of men in full-body swimsuits next to some wooden bathing huts, getting ready to swim in the river (two activities that never happen here now). This sprouted all sorts of conversations about changing fashions (why did people cover their bodies more?), how people spent their leisure time then, and whether we could try taking our dinghy down the river!

As we crossed the road back to our house, my daughter took my hand and said, 'We wouldn't have to check for cars now if we were in the old days. We'd just listen for clip, clop, clip, clop.'

TIP: Don't show your children the books and photos at all until you are out on your walk – keep them 'fresh'!

 IF YOU LIKE THIS, YOU MIGHT LIKE...PIN-IN-THE-MAP SKETCHING P.42

ART WITH A TWIST!

Quirky and engaging ways to get them absorbed in art

- Secret Cupboard Art
- Communal Art BRAVE + BOLD!
- Pin-in-the-map Sketching
- Butterfly Collector
- Russian Doll Roulette
- An 'Unsensible' Pair of Shoes
- Glow-in-the-dark Drawing Wall
- Snapshot of a Day

Secret Cupboard Art

Throw open some cupboard doors and let your kids create hidden works of art

Age: 4-13

What you need:

- Inside of a cupboard door
- Art materials

A bit of background

When we first moved to our current house, as soon as we got the keys, we ran around excitedly, exploring - opening cupboard doors, flicking switches, discovering nooks, climbing in crannies...

My (then) three-year old son was very pleased when he discovered on the inside of the under stairs cupboard door a child's picture of a monster-come-human creature with the message 'Please look after me.'

It was made with paint, bits of paper, sticky tape and string applied directly onto the door. It was very old and faded and had obviously been done by the previous owner's children, now grown up, who had sold the house to us. It triggered this idea.

Once children are old enough to hold a crayon, sooner or later they'll scribble on the furniture or a wall. To them, that carefully chosen, newly painted, 'Hint of sage' living room wall is just a huge, tempting, blank canvas. We adults get to paint, decorate and finish our houses down to the last detail but our children are expected to be hands off. But... the inside of cupboard doors...that's another matter. They are out of view most of the time, and when we do open them they don't enhance our life in any way.

What to do

So why not choose the inside of a cupboard door (airing, coats, under stairs, kitchen, wardrobe...) and let your children loose on it? Give them paints, pens, fabrics, tape, papers, glue, googly eyes – whatever you feel is right for the age they're at – and let them create a hidden piece of art. It's extra exciting for them because it feels mischievous and reckless to be doing art on a real grown-up

cupboard door. And from now on, it'll be there to amuse you every time you open it.

It'll also be a lasting memory of their 'art stage' at that age too. And, if you ever move house, it'll be there to surprise the next inhabitants!

AND ANOTHER IDEA...

Cupboard Hideout: Clear out a large cupboard (even temporarily) for young children to turn into a secret den. Give them torches and let them personalize the inside with rugs, cushions, soft toys...

 IF YOU LIKE THIS, YOU MIGHT LIKE...THE IRONING-BOARD HAIR WASH P.96

Communal Art

Invite everyone who comes to your door to be a small part of a big whole – and end up with a striking piece of art

Age: 5 to grown-up

What you need:

- Large art canvas
- Paints
- String
- Visitors (and patience!)

A bit of background

One cold, dark, frosty winter's evening, we went to an outdoor art festival in Oxford. I noticed a long line of children waiting to do something. Curious, I wandered up to the front of the queue. There was an artist with a huge, blank canvas on an easel and lots of different coloured pots of paint. Each pot had a piece of string submerged in it. One by one, she was getting each child to choose a paint colour, take the string out of it and throw it at the canvas! She then peeled the string carefully off and put it back in the paint pot. It sounds nursery-school simple, but it was gradually building up a delicious, aesthetically pleasing tangle of lines and curves and drips that made a really effective and sophisticated piece of art!

That would be really fun for the kids to do at home as a 'communal' art project, I thought. Every time someone came to our house over the next month or two – friends, neighbours or relatives – they could ask them to do a bit of string throwing! The children thought it was a great idea.

What we did

I got a large canvas (about 1m x 1m) and prepared six or seven pots of different colour paint (I used yoghurt pots filled with cheap poster paint and cling film over the top). I put a piece of string (about 12-15 cm long) in each pot. You could choose a limited palette of colours that go well together like purples, blues and pinks, but we went for a riot of uncoordinated colours. I put the canvas on an easel (but anywhere you can prop it up roughly at eye level will do).

Now every time there was a knock at the door, the kids got excited and leapt into action. Everyone who did it, children and adults, loved it. It added a little unexpected quirk to their day and they enjoyed being part of something bigger (they were all keen to see how it would turn out in the end). And it didn't matter if they were artistic or not – anyone can throw a piece of string!

The result ☆

Before too long, we had a very unusual, modern and head-turning piece of art – with a history: Those pink drips were made by Ollie when he came for tea after school, that really nice pale blue 'S' shape was Jennifer from next door when she came to borrow an onion…

If you're feeling really game, let the children ask the postman to step in and have a go, or the person who comes to read the gas meter!

 TIPS: For the best results. The string should be covered but not dripping with paint. Stand about 1.5m from the canvas when you throw. Don't throw the string with too much force!

SAME BUT DIFFERENT: Other communal art projects: How about giving visitors to your house a small square of paper and asking them to draw a quick self-portrait and sign their name? Put all the squares together to make a quirky picture of lots of people you know!

 IF YOU LIKE THIS, YOU MIGHT LIKE…THE DINNER PARTY EXPERIMENT P.20

Pin-in-the-map Sketching

**Do some art outdoors – but let chance decide
where you will go and what you will draw!**

What you need:

- A car
- A UK road atlas or ordnance survey map
  of your area
- A pin
- Sketch pads (or paper and something to lean on)
- Pencils, rubbers, pencil-sharpener etc.

A bit of background

When you see an artist working outside, they've usually chosen a spot where they can paint a scene or landmark they know and like. But outdoor art is much more appealing to kids if you take away all control over the destination! They'll produce an unpredictable piece and you might even discover a local nook and cranny you didn't know about before.

What we did

One sunny autumn day, we took our UK road atlas and turned it to the page that has the town where we live in on it. We got my daughter to close her eyes and stick a pin in it randomly. Curiously, when we looked, the point that she had jabbed was inside an area marked *Busford Park*. We'd never heard of it – was it a leafy park, a housing estate, or something else entirely? We jumped in the car

with sketch pads, freshly-sharpened pencils, camping chairs and a flask of soup, and drove until we found the exact spot. My 12-year-old son was given the challenge of navigating which added to his enjoyment.

We were pleasantly surprised to discover that Busford Park was in fact a stately home. Its grand gates were open enticingly, but the sign stated it was closed for winter. So we set up just outside the gates instead. The challenge, for all of us, was to draw the best picture we could from that spot. We each chose to draw an entirely different view. My son did a very technical, architectural picture of one of the gatehouses. I drew the other gatehouse. My husband sketched the elegant, tree-lined avenue leading up to the house and my daughter, facing away from the house, also decided to draw trees in various stages of Autumn fallout with some added fantasy elements of her own — like fairies climbing the trees and floating on the clouds!

The result ☆

We were all totally engrossed in our drawings and silent for a good 40 minutes. There was another twenty minutes adding details and comparing pictures. At one point, a woman in uniform (a maid?) came through the gates. She stopped to peer over our shoulders at our pictures.

'Interesting,' she commented.

> **TIP**: Don't forget to take something to sit on!

☞ IF YOU LIKE THIS, YOU MIGHT LIKE...HANSEL AND GRETEL WALK P.32

Butterfly Collector

Produce a beautiful and attention-grabbing butterfly collection – without any cruelty to animals!

What you need:

- Printouts of butterflies with their names from the Internet (or a book of butterflies)
- Paper, pencils, rubbers, felt-tip pens/coloured pencils/paints
- Scissors
- Box frame
- Pins with bobbles on the end

Age: 4-13

A bit of background

I love the image of children with nets running through a meadow of wild flowers on a summer's day catching butterflies. Butterflies are so beautiful and so ephemeral, you can't help but have an urge to chase them, catch them, pin them down and frame them forever. But that, of course, would be cruel and wrong!

When my daughter was learning about mini-beasts at school, she would come home talking animatedly about antennae and thoraxes and hind wings and was very excited about her trip to a butterfly house. It gave me the idea to do a bit of our own butterfly collecting – the kind way!

What we did

First we printed out pictures of lots of types of gorgeous, colourful butterflies from around the world from the Internet (with their Latin and common names). A book of butterflies from the library would do just as well. Then we sat around the kitchen table (though there's no need for adults to join in) with blank white paper and a choice of felt-tipped pens, paints and coloured pencils.

We chose two of the butterflies each to copy as carefully as we could – roughly the same size as real butterflies. For my husband this meant reproducing a near-perfect, extremely realistic *Plain Tiger* and a *Monarch*. For my 4-year-old daughter it meant drawing and colouring a rather approximate (!) but commendable effort of an *Orange Tip* and a *Comma*. My son's and mine were somewhere in between in standard but everyone was quiet and fully absorbed.

When our butterflies were finished we cut them out carefully and bent them in the middle so that the wings were raised slightly like a real butterfly's. We took a box frame we had bought especially, and cut a piece of paper the right size to fit it. Then we used pins (the type with the bobbles at the end) to pin each of the butterflies to the paper. We typed out their Latin and common names and glued these as labels underneath each butterfly – for that authentic museum feel!

The result ☆

Now our butterfly collection sits on our kitchen windowsill. At first glance it looks exactly like a Victorian collection of real butterflies. Visitors are drawn to it. Only as you get close up, can you see that actually the butterflies are made of paper and hand-made! The more butterflies you can create, the bigger and more effective your collection will be. In fact, this project would work fantastically with a large group of children. Or you could even ask every visitor to your house to choose and reproduce a butterfly until you have a huge collection!

My daughter enjoyed it so much that after we'd finished, she started to design and colour her own made-up butterflies, inventing names for them like *Pinky Tips* and *Magic Flutterby*.

TIPS: Your butterfly collection will look even better if you make it look old and musty! To get that vintage look, rub the piece of paper you are going to pin the butterflies to with strong (liquid) coffee unevenly. Rub the box frame with dark wood stain. And when you type out the names, choose a font that looks like old typewriter writing!

☞ IF YOU LIKE THIS, YOU MIGHT LIKE...HAMSTER PLAYGROUND P.68

Russian Doll Roulette

**This art project involves Russian dolls and random people!
Set it in motion – then wait and see the results.**

What you need:

- Set of blank Russian dolls
- Envelopes
- Stamps
- Paper, a pen

A bit of background

Have you ever seen those sets of nesting Russian dolls that are completely blank – just plain wood – ready for you to paint yourself in your own design? You can get them in some toyshops or online quite cheaply. Well I decided to buy a set of them. But here's the twist! The children weren't going to paint them, nor was I! We'd separate the set of seven dolls and post each one in a parcel to a different person, asking them to paint it in any way they liked and send it back to us. We would be the lucky recipients!

What we did

I discussed with the children which seven of our friends and family we should send them to. We ended up choosing a mixture of adults and children, and a mixture of people we knew were arty and people who'd said things like 'I haven't got an artistic bone in my body' – but that we thought would secretly enjoy the challenge! We also thought carefully about what size doll to send each person (the small ones are more fiddly to do). Then we opened up each doll and tucked instructions like these inside:

Dear ....

Welcome to our unusual art project! We would love it if you could paint this Russian Doll – in any way you like. It could be a person, a character, an animal or even a self-portrait! When you've finished, please sign your name on the bottom and send it back to us in the SAE. It will be added to the other Russian Dolls in the set being painted by other random people to make a rather special collection!

Thank you!

Love ....

Then we posted them off in little parcels with a SAE and waited in anticipation. It was so exciting for the children (and me!) to receive the parcels back in the post one by one over the coming months and see the results. Now we have a really quirky set of Russian dolls on display in our living room, with a lot of personal meaning: Auntie Molly did that one, that one's by Mikey...

SAME BUT DIFFERENT:

Reverse it: Have your own family paint one Russian doll each as a self-portrait and sign their name on the bottom. Then give the whole set as a birthday or Christmas present to a grandparent.

AND ANOTHER IDEA...

Jigsaw Roulette:

Buy a child's jigsaw from a charity shop with very large pieces. Paint them with Gesso (see page 48 for Gesso reference) and send them out to different people. Ask each person to paint it according to a particular theme or colour scheme e.g. animals, flowers, orange, yellow and red colours. When you get all the pieces back, do the jigsaw and frame it!

 IF YOU LIKE THIS, YOU MIGHT LIKE...COMMUNAL ART P.40, REVERSE TRICK OR TREATING P.124

An 'Unsensible' Pair of Shoes

Turn an ordinary shoe into something extraordinary!

What you need:

- Old shoes (one per person)
- Art and craft materials

Age: 5-13

A bit of background

I heard about a friend of a friend who was doing a Foundation Arts course. Her pre-course task over the summer was to take a shoe – any shoe – and artify and customize it in anyway she liked. Apparently she gave her's wheels!

That sounded to me like something that would be very appealing to children! There's something really satisfying about taking a real-life, functional, 3D object and transforming it into 'art' so that it's interesting to look at – or even unrecognizable. My son, who often tells me that he isn't good at art was really taken with this idea.

What we did

I bought two pairs of shoes from a car boot sale in very different styles: One pair was bright pink with 5-inch heels, the other brown, flat and grannyish with a bow. The four of us gathered around the table (though you could set this up for kids to do

on their own) with a huge pile of arty bits and pieces like fabric, feathers, pom-poms, buttons, glue, tissue paper, sequins, twigs, papers, an old map, paint, ink stamps, old bits of metal and other found objects. Then we each chose a shoe and began.

The result ☆

My son took a masculine, technical approach and decided to turn his into a kind of 'shoe-car' with wheels salvaged from his old toy cars. He painted it white, decorated the inside with pieces of road map and covered the outside with graffiti by stamping it with random words. My finished product looked like some sort of Tudor torture contraption with old springs, a broken zip, hooks and metallic buttons. My daughter's had a stripy heel, spots and sparkly stars and was fur lined for a luxurious look. And my husband's was surprisingly feminine, completely covered in small, intricate, orange, yellow and red tissue paper swirls. Lined up and displayed on a shelf, they looked like part of a wacky art exhibition – or an odd shoe museum.

The question was, would any of us dare to wear a pair of those shoes out?

 TIPS: There are two magic tools for projects like this, both of which you can buy in art shops:

1. Gesso: This is a white, opaque primer that will adhere to any surface (wood, metal, shoes!) and provide a base that you can paint on top of with ordinary paint.

2. A hot glue gun: This makes sticking things to objects really easy (but be careful young children don't burn themselves with it).

 AND ANOTHER IDEA...

Pimp your Flip Flops: Get a really cheap pair of simple flip flops and customize the thongs with sequins, pompoms, bits of fabric wound round... Then wear them through the summer.

IF YOU LIKE THIS, YOU MIGHT ALSO LIKE...IF YOU GO DOWN TO THE WOODS TODAY P.58

Glow-in-the-dark Drawing Wall

Art in the dark drawings that glow and then disappear. This easy-to-make magic wall is great fun!

Age: 3-10

What you need:

- Glow-in-the-dark paint
- UV LED torches

A bit of background

One Saturday we visited a small, hands-on, science museum. One of the most popular exhibits was a 'glow-in-the-dark' wall inside a darkened room. Children could use a special light pen to create drawings and writing in flowing, fluorescent, mesmerising lines which gradually faded away.

I wondered how they made such a wall and if it would be possible to make one at home. So I emailed the museum to ask them and received a personal reply from the scientist who'd made it! He told me that it would actually be very easy to make one at home. All I needed to do was paint a wall with glow-in-the-dark paint in a space that was very dark in the evenings. Then the children could point a UV LED torch close up to it to draw and write. He said most types would work – for example, those used to check that bank notes aren't fake – but that I should avoid the 3-in-1 types.

What we did

I ordered some regular, green, glow-in-the-dark paint online and a couple of UV LED torches (I went for the very small keychain type as they were cheapest). I chose to paint a panel of the wooden balustrade along the landing. That space was out of the way and it was really dark there in the evenings with the lights off. You should choose a matt, white or cream surface – it won't work well over colour or gloss. A section of wall in a child's bedroom would be a great place!

Mark out the area you want to paint with masking tape and do three or four coats for the best results. I found that 60ml covered an area of about 70 x 70 cm, but you could make your's bigger or smaller than this. The good thing is that afterwards, the painted surface doesn't really look any different in the daytime – so you could probably get away with doing this even in rented accommodation!

That evening my daughter had a friend round for tea. I gave them the torches, turned the light out and they covered the area in squiggly lines, flowers, stars, hearts, their names... Then we turned the torches off to see the full, glow effect in the dark. A few minutes later the lines had disappeared and it was a blank canvas ready for the girls to use all over again!

I even used it to write some sums on, the challenge being for them to work out the answers before they faded away!

TIP: The best time to make your glow-in-the-dark wall is in the winter when it gets dark early. Then the children will have plenty of time to use it before bedtime!

BEWARE! Make sure the children are supervised and that they know to ONLY shine the torches at the wall. The human eye cannot detect UV light so it can be very damaging.

 IF YOU LIKE THIS, YOU MIGHT LIKE...SHRUNKEN HEADS P.118

Snapshot of a Day

A special art project that will capture the moment and trigger precious memories in years to come!

What you need:

- Paper, pencil, coloured pencils felt-tip pens
- Paints and brushes
- Frame

A bit of background

Are you bored with the school run? Making packed lunches? Nagging your kids to get dressed? The bedtime routine? These things seem ordinary and mundane – even tedious – to us right now, but in years to come, the day-in-day out stuff may be the memories we treasure the most. When your kids are grown-up, you almost certainly won't remember that your son wanted marmite and peanut butter sandwiches in his lunch box every single day when he was 8, or that your daughter refused to wear anything but the yellow dress with the dragonfly on the front when she was 5!

What we did

Here's a fun, interesting project for your children to do that will 'capture' the details of everyday life and produce a quirky piece of art that will become more and more valuable as the years go by. Take these two projects that we did as examples:

What I ate today by Fred, age 8½
I took a bird's eye photo of *everything* my son ate on one ordinary school day - breakfast, morning snack, packed lunch, after-school snack and dinner (he was a big eater – still is! – and it was rather a phenomenal amount of food!). I gave my son the photos and a large piece of paper and explained that he was going to make a 'memory-maker' picture – a bit like a time capsule, but 2D! I set him the task of copying the food from the photos, colouring/painting them and then labeling the meals (breakfast, packed lunch…) and the items (porridge with jam, kiwi fruit…). I encouraged him to add small, personal annotations too, like 'I like the yellow bit of the egg best' and 'This is my favourite fruit. My second favourite fruit is strawberries'. Finally, he headed it with the title *What I ate today by Fred, age 8 ½* and the date. It resulted in an unusual and very engaging painting which I framed to keep forever!

My favourite clothes by Lola, age 5 ¾
My daughter and I rummaged through her bedroom for her absolute favourite clothes – the ones she liked to wear again and again. (She wanted to include her favourite dressing-up shoes and her swimming costume too). I laid them all out flat on the living room floor and again, gave her a large piece of paper and set her the task of drawing them all and annotating them. ('This is my party dress. My friend Ruby gave it to me.'). She loved drawing all her pretty, girly clothes and stripy tights. Finally, she titled it *My favourite clothes by Lola, age 5 ¾*, with the date. Another one to frame and treasure!

Other possibilities are:

- An annotated map of the walk to school (friend's houses, blackberry bushes etc.)
- A bird's eye view of the play park you visit the most (swings, see-saw etc.)
- Favourite toys and/or cuddly toys

TIP: After a while, hide the picture away somewhere, like in the loft, to be brought out in many years to come. It will have become incredibly interesting and precious!

 SAME BUT DIFFERENT:

Film it: You could make a film 'An ordinary day in the life of (name of child)'. It could include waking up, breakfast, the walk to school, and so on, with your child giving their commentary.

 IF YOU LIKE THIS, YOU MIGHT LIKE...NEW YEAR'S INTERVIEW P.122

DESIGN AND CONSTRUCTION

Inventive projects for designing and making in a 'real life' way

- DIY Marble Run
- If You Go Down to the Woods Today...
- Newspaper Clothes
- Tick, Tock, Tick, Tock...
- Dress Me Up! BRAVE + BOLD!
- Mini Interior Designer
- Hamster Playground

DIY Marble Run

There are lots of different marble runs you can buy, but it's even more fun to create your own impromptu one

Age: 6 to grown-up

What you need:

- Marbles
- Duct tape
- Cardboard and plastic boxes, packets, tubes, etc.

A bit of background

If you're the type of parent who likes making complicated wooden train set layouts, or the bit at the beginning of *Thunderbirds* where Virgil Tracey goes down various interconnecting chutes to end up in the driving seat of Thunderbird 2, you'll love this idea!

What we did

We dug out from our recycling boxes all the boxes, cardboard tubes, plastic bottles, milk cartons and anything else that might be useful in making a marble run. We looked for interesting shapes and bits that we thought would work well and cut them up.

Here are some ideas to get you going:

- Cut off the long corner edges of cereal or other big boxes to make V-shaped ramps
- Use kitchen and toilet rolls whole or cut in half lengthways as chutes
- The top halves of plastic bottles and plastic milk cartons turned upside down (without the lid) are good for marbles to plop through vertically
- Use the tubes from wrapping paper and foil as tunnels. You can make a small marble-size hole near the end for the marble to fall through
- Cut slits in both sides of a toilet roll to make an elbow bend to go round a corner
- Make zig-zag chutes for the marble to roll downwards from one diagonal chute to the next

We wanted to make the longest marble run in the world (!), so we started upstairs at the far end of our landing and worked our way along it, round the corner, down the banister, round the corner again and along to the kitchen – a total of 9 metres! (It'll be even more fun if you live in a three-floor house. If you live in a bungalow you can start from the top of some high furniture). We stuck the pieces in place with duct tape, against the banister and stairs and put a fruit punnet at the very bottom ready to collect all the marbles.

The children became more and more creative and absorbed in its construction and by the second half, I had been relegated to tape hander-over only! Their pièce de résistance was an impressive fast-spinning plughole effect that they created – by chance – with the top section of an old smoothie bottle.

Two-and-a-half hours later, we all squealed with pleasure and satisfaction when we rolled the first marble from the very top to the very bottom successfully!

'I wish I could shrink myself and slide down it!' said my son.

AND ANOTHER IDEA...

Masking Tape Roads:
Use masking tape to make an appealing (temporary!) network of roads on the floor where little ones can play with their toy cars. You could use two lines of tape to show the edges of the road and small strips like road markings down the middle of the road. It works on hard floors or carpets.

TIPS:
• Secure everything really firmly in place with the tape.

• Test each part of the marble run as you go along by rolling a marble down it.

• Use gentle rather than steep slopes or the marble will fly off.

 IF YOU LIKE THIS, YOU MIGHT LIKE...GLOW-IN-THE-DARK DRAWING WALL P.50

If You Go Down to the Woods Today...

Photograph your teddies in real life situations and turn it into a story book

What you need:

- Soft toys
- Camera
- Computer
- Printer, paper and card
- Stapler, glue and pens

A bit of background

When my son was in the Beavers, whenever one of the group went on holiday, they were given Bertie the beaver (a soft toy) to take with them and photograph on location. We have a great photo of him against the backdrop of the Eiffel Tower!

Flicking through the photograph album of that holiday one day with my (then) 6-year old daughter, it triggered a thought. 'Hey, we could do that,' I said to her. 'Take photos of your teddies outside or around the house doing *real* things.' 'Yes!' she said enthusiastically. 'And then make a book out of it!'

What we did

That Saturday she chose four of her favourite soft toys to be the stars: Two large teddies called Belinda and Honey Bear, Ella the Elephant and Bluebell the Reindeer. Then she set about staging them in various realistic situations.

The possibilities are endless, but she put the teddies:

- At the kitchen table eating dinner with – she insisted – wine (water and red food colouring) for the mummy and daddy bear
- On the sofa, one with a mug of tea, one with the remote control and two reading books (*We're going on a Bear hunt!* and *Teach yourself Turkish*)!
- Loading the washing machine
- Playing draughts
- Cooking at the cooker with saucepan and wooden spoon
- In goggles and (her) swimming costume ready for a swimming lesson

- Looking in the fridge
- At the computer
- Washing their hands at the sink
- Tucked up in (her) bed

We also went to the park down the road and set them up having a picnic under a tree!

The result ☆

I took lots of photos and later printed out the best ones of each situation onto ordinary paper. The results were very effective! (My favourite was one of Belinda on the toilet!). We made a blank book by stapling paper together with card for the cover and I left her to it, gluing the pictures in and writing the story.

An hour or so later, she'd produced *Busy Bears* which told the full story of the teddies' day from morning until bedtime. She'd even written a blurb on the back!

AND ANOTHER IDEA...

Teddy Doctor: A simple box of plasters can keep young children amused for quite a while (it takes them a bit of time just to open each one!). Let them stick them all over their dolls, teddies and each other!

TIPS:

• Props make all the difference to the photos. Reading (or other glasses) on a teddy have a great effect! You could also use doll's or baby clothes, watches, headphones, straws for drinks...

• Sometimes one of you will need to hold the teddy in place, staying hidden from the view off the camera e.g. at the bathroom sink or at the cooker.

 IF YOU LIKE THIS, YOU MIGHT LIKE...DON'T FORGET TO SMELL THE FLOWERS P.28

Newspaper Clothes

How much pleasure can you get out of a pile of old newspapers? Quite a lot, if you use them to make outfits with!

(although children under 8 will probably need to be the models rather than the tailors)

What you need:

- Old newspapers
- Scissors and sticky tape

A bit of background

When I was in my early 20s, pre-kids, I once threw a 'Red party' where I invited everyone to come wearing something red. I remember one guy came in an outfit made entirely out of newspaper. 'That's not red,' I said to him. 'Yes, it is,' he replied, 'Black and white and read all over!'

Years later, with kids, I had a flashback to that party and thought, we could have a bash at that... a spot of newspaper fashion design!'. As it turned out, it's actually quite astonishing the clothes you can make out of newspaper and how good they look.

What we did

Armed with a stack of old newspapers, scissors and sticky tape, we split into pairs (dad-son and mum-daughter in our case). One person was to be the 'tailor' and the other person the 'model' – and assistant to the tailor. The aim was for each pair to make a complete outfit out of newspaper.

There were no rules and no special techniques – except that measuring worked best by wrapping the newspaper round the model to gauge size or having the model lie down and drawing round their body. However, we did go into separate rooms so that we couldn't copy ideas from each other and so we could surprise each other at the end with our creations!

After much discussion, fitting, snipping, folding and taping, we had two rather dashing outfits! My son was wearing trousers, a tank top and a bow tie and my daughter was in a dress with fringed bottom and front pockets. But there really is no limit to what you can make: Dresses, waistcoats, mini-skirts, hats and even shoes! If you add details like flares, belts, pleats, braces, collars and necklaces too, it's even more effective.

The result ☆

When we'd finished, we had our models walk up and down the catwalk (living room rug) strutting their stuff and striking poses while the camera flashed!

 AND ANOTHER IDEA...

Paint your clothes: Did you know you can use ordinary, cheap, acrylic paint to permanently dye clothes? Take a few colours, water them down, give the kids some paintbrushes and let them completely cover an old white T-shirt or pillowcase in their own designs. Much more fun and flowing than fabric paint!

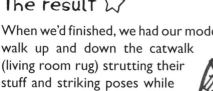

 IF YOU LIKE THIS, YOU MIGHT LIKE...AN 'UNSENSIBLE' PAIR OF SHOES P.48

Tick Tock, Tick Tock...

Create an around-the-world collection of clocks – and keep the big wide world in your children's consciousness!

Age: 5-13

What you need:

- A number of clocks (unlimited!)
- Paints and paintbrushes
- Glue and craft materials

A bit of background

I attended a workshop at the Indian YMCA in London one day, where the majority of guests were Indian. Sitting in the lobby, I noticed two clocks with different times on the wall: one labelled London and one labelled India.

Now since my daughter is adopted from China, it gave me the idea to put two clocks in her bedroom, one set to English time (labelled 'England') and one set to Chinese time (labelled 'China'). We try to keep her country and family of origin fresh in her mind, and this way, we could refer to the clocks. For instance, in the morning:

Chinese children will be coming home from school about now. So that's what I did.

However, my son (who is not adopted) liked the idea too and suggested a 'Hungary' clock because that's where his best friend is from. And why not a 'Turkey' clock where we had just been on holiday? And so the clocks multiplied...

What we did

We collected a variety of wall clocks from charity shops and car boot sales – the more random in style the better! Then the kids got stuck in

Japan

Great britain.

America.

customizing the clocks with paint and craft materials – to make each clock unique and interesting. They painted stripes, spots and patterns on the frames and glued on stars, feathers, pom-poms, sequins, strings of beads dangling down, pipe cleaners coiled like alien antennae and other quirky details!

We ended up with a very colourful, wacky collection of clocks ready to put up on their bedroom wall. They decided which countries they wanted to represent and printed out the names to be stuck underneath each clock. (If you're a family that likes travelling, you could create a clock for each country that you have visited and keep adding them.) We put the clocks in a line, working from East to West – to make it more obvious whether the time was a.m or p.m. But you could arrange them anyhow and anywhere you like. On the wall going up the stairs would be fun, or perhaps in a toilet – something to ponder when you're on the loo!

All they had to do then was check time zones on the Internet and set each clock to the right time.

The clocks definitely keep the wider world in the children's minds, initiating conversations about the location of countries, the earth's rotation, flights, jet lag, the International Date Line, whether you can travel backwards or forwards in time... They look pretty good too!

 TIP: Two things which are very useful for this and other similar projects are gesso and a hot glue gun (see p.49 for more information on these)

SAME BUT DIFFERENT: **Countrified Clocks**: You could customize each clock in a way that suits that country. A 'Japan' clock decorated with origami, Indian braid round the edge of the 'India' clock, red, white and blue for the 'Britain' clock.

france...

Holland.

 IF YOU LIKE THIS, YOU MIGHT LIKE...THE DAY OF THE CHOPSTICKS P.18

Dress Me Up!

Would you dare to let your children choose and buy you an outfit that you have to wear the rest of the day?!

Age: 10 to grown-up

What you need:

- A big cheap clothes shop
- Money (set a budget!)

A bit of background

My son doesn't like the way I dress. He has never liked it. When he was only five, not long after he'd started school, he said to me, 'Why don't you dress like the other mummies?' 'What do you mean?' I replied, a bit taken aback. 'Well, your clothes are different...sort of, well, like...' he said, struggling to describe (I think!) the fact that I quite like colourful, ethnic clothes. I felt a little hurt, but it led – eventually – to this idea.

What we did

When he was 11, I told him I was going to take him shopping and let him choose and buy me an outfit – anything he wanted! Then I would wear those clothes for the rest of the day. In public!

He pounced on the idea with relish – and even if your child is happy with the way you dress, I bet they'd love the chance to re-invent you. I was a little nervous but I reckoned he wouldn't make me look deliberately ridiculous if he had got to walk around with me wearing them. So we headed off to one of those really huge clothes shops where he could browse and choose clothes cheaply all under the one roof. 'How did you spend your Saturday, Fred?' I heard him snigger to himself, '...in a ladies clothes shop!'

So, what did he choose for me?

- A dark blue floral blouse
  He said: *I like the way the sleeves are all flouncy.*
  I thought: *Nasty fabric, the sort of thing an old lady might wear to a wedding.*
- Some dark, indigo blue jeans, with artificially worn-out white patches at the front of the thighs.
  He said: *The white bits are fashionable.*
  I thought: *The white bits look naff.*
- Some white flip-flops with a pattern of tiny cherries on them.
  He said: *I like the cherries.*
  I thought: *They look prim and 'housewifely'.*

- A chunky plastic bracelet
  He said: *You should wear more of this type of jewellery.*
  I thought: *It's ghastly. Ugly and cheap looking.*

However, I kept my mouth zipped and headed off obediently to the changing rooms. I was supremely embarrassed even just walking back along the aisle to the doorway to show my son. He gave me a look of triumph and a thumbs up. We bought the lot!

I changed into the outfit and ventured out into the world. I felt ridiculous! When I caught a glimpse of myself in shop windows and mirrors, it was like seeing my head on someone else's body! But it made me laugh and that made him laugh and we had a very giggly, upbeat afternoon. We went for lunch, to the library, to the shops and thankfully, we didn't bump into a single person I knew!

When we get home, my husband killed himself laughing. 'You look like somebody with a completely different character!' he said.

'So,' I said to my son, 'Shall I pick you up from school on Monday wearing this?' 'No way,' he said, alarmed. 'Don't you dare. Everyone would stare at you!'

SAME BUT DIFFERENT:
Charity shop dress-up:
You could go around charity shops choosing the clothes instead. It'll make the choice of clothes more challenging, but even more interesting!

 IF YOU LIKE THIS, YOU MIGHT LIKE...THE UNSCARY SCARECROW P.114

Mini Interior Designer

From wallpaper to curtains to clocks – give your children an empty house to decorate and furnish from scratch

What you need:

- Wooden CD storage unit with compartments (often found at car boot sales or charity shops)
- Craft and junk materials
- Glue (a hot glue gun is very very handy)

Age: 5-13

A bit of background

I noticed that when my daughter played with her doll's house, one of the things she enjoyed the most was arranging and rearranging the furniture and adding home-made bits and bobs – like a rug made from a piece of paper, a duvet cover made from a scrap of fabric …

So when I saw an old wooden CD storage unit in the pile of stuff to take to the charity shop I suddenly saw it in a whole new light! It would make a fantastic miniature house – each compartment was like an empty room just waiting to be decorated and furnished. I'd give it to my daughter and let her inner interior designer go berserk!

What we did

I sawed it in half to reduce the number of compartments from eight to four so that there could be a living room, kitchen, bathroom and bedroom. Then I gathered together a whole bunch of crafty and junky stuff that could be used to make décor and furniture.

For example, you could use:

- Wrapping paper for wallpaper
- Fabric remnants for curtains and rugs
- Lolly sticks to make window frames
- Small boxes, packaging, balsa wood and twigs to make furniture
- Cut up greeting cards to make art for the walls
- One of those dunking cream cheese and breadsticks containers as a bath
- Photos of clocks/fires/fridges and so on cut from catalogues to stick on walls
- Matchboxes as drawers
- Individual hollows of egg boxes to make funky chairs
- Foil for mirrors

In fact, once you get into the miniature world mindset, you start seeing everything around you in terms of how it could be used in the house! I couldn't

Caution!
(the boring but necessary bit!)

Obviously, hamsters are not toys. To make sure they stay safe and healthy:

- Use plain, brown cardboard boxes and packaging which does not have colour or text printed on it. Remove any plastic wrapping. Don't use paint.

- Make sure all the tape is firmly pressed down and that the sticky side is not exposed anywhere.

- Make sure there are no sharp edges or holes/tunnels of a size the hamster could get stuck in.

- Don't make anything so high that the hamster would hurt itself if it fell.

- Don't leave the hamster in the playground for too long. 1) It might get hungry and thirsty. 2) It would chew its way out eventually.

- Don't put hamsters together in the playground which do not normally live together in the same cage.

- Don't put the hamster in the playground if there's a cat around!

TIP: Put some tasty treats in the playground dotted about here and there to encourage the hamster to explore (and make them feel secure).

Wheee!

 IF YOU LIKE THIS, YOU MIGHT LIKE...DIY MARBLE RUN P.56

CHINWAGGERS

Unique and stimulating ideas to really get them talking

- Graph of the Day
- Story Dice
- Pants on Fire!

Graph of the Day

An engaging, cosy, one-to-one activity – that'll trick your child into telling you *everything* about their day at school!

What you need:

- Pen and paper
- One to one time

A bit of background

Like most parents, extracting information from my children about how their day at school was – especially from my son – is pretty painful! I usually get a one-word response such as 'Fine' or 'Okay' and further probing like 'What did you have for school dinner?' or 'What did you do in PE?' only leads to a 'Can't remember' or a 'Dunno'. It can be pretty frustrating – after all, they spend 6 hours at school, 5 days a week, 39 weeks of the year! Not only am I interested to know more about their life-without-me, sometimes there are things I'm concerned about and want to check on.

Then I came up with an idea that turned the post-school conversation from a blood-out-of-a-stone exercise into an enjoyable experience for each child that got lots and lots of juicy details out of them!

What you do

The best time to do this activity is close to bedtime, when your child is relaxed – and rather surprised and pleased that you want to do something with them when they're about to go to bed! It makes them extra forthcoming!

Tell your child you are going to make a 'Graph of their day' together. Snuggle up somewhere with a piece of paper and a pen. Draw a vertical axis and

mark it 1 to 10 going upwards. Draw a horizontal axis and jot along it the main things your child has done that day, starting with the morning and working through the day. For example: assembly, literacy, maths, playtime... ballet, friend's house for tea.

Now, ask them to give a score out of 10 for how they felt during each of those parts of the day – where 10 is absolutely fantastic and 1 is downright terrible. Put a dot in the right place on the graph. After each score, ask them why it gets that score – especially if something gets a really low or a really high score. You might discover, for instance, that playtime only gets a 1 because they felt they had no one to play with, or that the afternoon lesson gets a 10 because they got to try Spanish food and they loved it. Finally, let them join the dots up to make a line graph of the highs and lows of their day!

It's a chance to connect, find out what they're feeling, discover what they're enjoying and not enjoying at school, and to discuss anything that's bothering them. Your child goes to bed happy and satisfied, having reflected on their day, shared any problems and had your full attention. And you find out lots. Everyone's a winner!

Even my son responds really well to this. While he isn't usually that open or articulate when talking about his feelings, he finds the concrete, mathematical and fun approach of the 'Graph of the Day' non-threatening and rather appealing!

 TIP: Listen to your child long and hard before you jump in with your responses, opinions, advice or judgements! You'll get a lot more out of them!

 SAME BUT DIFFERENT:

Graph of the Trip:
If your child has been away (e.g. Scout camp, a school residential trip, a stay with relatives), get them to give a score for each day and find out what really went on!

Reverse it! Let your child make a graph of *your* day sometimes too! How often do they get to find out the full details of what you did while they were at school?

 IF YOU LIKE THIS, YOU MIGHT LIKE...SNAPSHOT OF A DAY P.52

Story Dice

Give simple wooden blocks a whole new dimension with this story-telling game

What you need:

- 4 toy blocks
- Paper and glue (or plain sticky labels)
- Felt-tipped pens

A bit of background

My daughter loved her little trolley of red, green, blue and yellow building blocks when she was a toddler but of course she quickly got to an age when she was beyond making towers and knocking them over.

I was about to pass them on to a friend with a one-year-old when I realized it would be easy to give them a whole new lease of life beyond the toddler years. I'd keep a few and turn them into a game which would spark imagination and creative thinking.

What I did

I took four of the blocks. Then I cut up some square pieces of paper which were just a tiny bit smaller than the sides of the blocks (you could use stickers instead). Onto each piece I drew a very simple picture. I needed one picture for each side of each block, so 24 (4 x 6) in total. To get ideas for pictures, it helped to think in categories:

Animals: cat, giraffe, penguin…
People: boy, witch, nurse…
Transport: plane, tractor, hot air balloon…
Clothes: wellies, pair of trousers, high-heeled shoes…
Food: egg, lollipop, fish and chips…
Nature: rainbow, mountain, tree…
Household objects: washing machine, umbrella, toothpaste…

Don't worry about making the pictures look good. You could get your kids to draw them or even use pictures cut from magazines – but they'll look more appealing if you use colour.

When I'd finished, I glued or stuck the pictures to the sides of the blocks until they were all covered. It works best if you keep to one or two categories for each block. For example, block 1 is animals and transport, block 2 is clothes and food, and so on.

Now we were ready to begin our story-telling game. Here's how it works. The first person throws the four story dice, one at a time. See which four pictures land face up. Now they must tell a short story which includes all four of those things (in any order) beginning 'Once upon a time…'.

It can be quite a challenge (have you ever tried to invent a story with a tractor, an ice-cream, a pair of socks and a tortoise in it?!) but that's what makes it fun. It teaches kids all sorts of things about what makes a good story – like beginnings, middles and ends, and creating and resolving a problem within a story – as well as thinking on your feet! And when you've exhausted those blocks, it's easy to make some more with fresh pictures.

The result ☆

My daughter, at the age of 4, absolutely loved it. I can even remember a camping trip where I was forced to play it bleary-eyed from my sleeping bag first thing in the morning!

Here's an example of one of her stories:
Dice throw: *Rabbit, rain, fairy, scooter*
Story: *Once upon a time there was a fairy. One day it started raining and her wings got really soggy and she couldn't fly any more. She felt really sad and started crying. Just then, along came a rabbit on a scooter. He said, 'Why are you crying little fairy?' She told him about her soggy wings. He said, 'I can help you. Jump on my scooter.' And he took her for a really fast ride on her scooter until the wind had dried her wings and they worked again ('cause it had stopped raining by then). She was so happy. And the rabbit and fairy were friends forever. The end.*

TIP: The story dice are a great take-anywhere toy! Keep them in your bag and use them on long car journeys, at restaurants, on holiday…

IF YOU LIKE THIS, YOU MIGHT LIKE…PICTURE TRAIL TREASURE HUNT P.90

Pants on Fire!

Lying is bad, lying is wrong, but it can also be really, really funny! Try this game and see.

What you need:

- Paper and pens
- A set of questions

A bit of background

We all try to teach our children not to lie, right? 'Don't tell fibs, honesty is the best policy, the boy who cried wolf…'

But, the thing is, telling porkie pies can be a hoot for children and adults. Here's a lying game I invented. It needs a little bit of preparation but it's well, well worth it.

What you do

You'll need two teams of equal numbers (but a minimum of two people on a team). I'll call them Team A and Team B here but we usually choose team names e.g. *Team Pinocchio*. Then you'll need to prepare a list of 10 questions. Here are some suggestions:

• What's the naughtiest thing you've ever done?

• What present would you most like for your next birthday?

• What do you like the most about your mum/dad?

• What would be your ideal day?

• What new hobby would you most like to try?

• What has been your most embarrassing moment?

• Which country would you most like to go to?

• Who do you most admire?

• What's your most treasured possession?

• What superpower would you like to have the most?

Give half the questions to Team A and half to Team B. All members of both teams then spend time preparing their individual answers to their questions (in their head or jotting down notes for themselves). BUT for each question one person on the team prepares a FALSE answer – a big fat whopper! – while the others tell the TRUTH. So the team will need to whisper and confer amongst themselves first to decide who is going to be 'the liar' for each question!

Now you can begin the game properly. Team A and Team B should sit by opposite each other. Start with Team A and their first question. Each team member takes it in turn to give their answer. Explain to everyone before you start that their answers should be like stories, anecdotal, with lots of detail and elaboration for authenticity. They can also use facial expression, darts of the eyes, hand gestures and body language to give the impression they are telling the truth (if they are lying) or lying (if they are telling the truth). Once you get really good at the game you can double bluff too and make it seem like you're lying when you are lying and telling the truth when you are telling the truth!

When all of Team A have given their answers to the question, Team B discuss who they think the liar is and announce it. If they get it right, they get a point. If they get it wrong, the other team get a point for tricking them successfully.

Now it's Team B's turn to give answers to their first question and so on...

You'll laugh a lot and learn things about each other you never knew. ('Mum, you really did that when you were a kid?!'). However, you do of course, risk your children honing their lying skills and getting rather good at it!

TIP: It's fun if each team member has two little cards folded over in half, one with a tick inside (= true) and one with a cross inside (= false). Then after the other team has guessed who is lying, the team can open their cards in unison and reveal in true TV quiz style who 'the liar' really is!

AND ANOTHER IDEA...

Operation Incognito: Invent completely new identities for yourselves, including names, hobbies, home town, pets... and go to another town. Spend all day calling each other by your fake names and referring to your fake lives. The more unusual they are, the more eavesdroppers will prick up their ears!

 IF YOU LIKE THIS, YOU'LL LIKE...DRESS ME UP! P.64

WORDSMITHS

Original and creative ways to experiment with the written word

- The Witch's Larder
- Word Towers
- Black-out Poems

The Witch's Larder

**Could your food cupboards do with a good sort out?
Your kids will be happy to help if you turn it
into a spooky re-naming activity!**

What you need:

- Pens
- Plain stickers

A bit of background

One day I decided my larder really had reached a point where it needed attention - dusty packets of unused lentils, spilt cornflakes and other general chaos. At this time, my daughter was into *Winnie the Witch* books and my son was studying the 'Double, double toil and trouble...' witches' speech from Macbeth at school.

So I thought we could combine a boring chore with a bit of imaginative fun for them. I told them we were going to turn the larder into a witch's larder full of weird and wonderful ingredients that she might put into her cauldron when she was making magic spells. I said I wanted them to look carefully at all the foods we had and invent new and revolting names for them like 'eye of newt', 'toe of frog', 'tongue of dog' and 'scale of dragon'. I'd give them pens and lots of plain white stickers to make labels which they could stick on the packets and jars.

What we did

Together, we emptied out the larder completely and spread the food all over the kitchen table ready for re-labelling. Then while I was cleaning and de-cluttering the larder, their brains got into gross-you-out mode!

Here are some of the new names they thought up:

Thai red curry paste: Monkey intestines

Kidney beans: Shrivelled kids' lungs

Ketchup: Congealed blood of cow

Marmalade: Jellied chicken beaks

Peppercorns: Shrunken rat's eyes

Vinegar: Dragon's saliva

Bisto: Dried baby maggots

Marmite: Melted parents (!)

It still brings a smile to my face now when I grab something from the back of the larder as I'm cooking and rediscover its 'witch's' name!

TIP: If you want to make the labels look old and musty, rub the stickers first with strong (liquid) coffee. You could even use those old-fashioned luggage labels with string to tie round the necks of jars and bottles. Again, rub them with coffee first.

AND ANOTHER IDEA...

All Eyes: Let your children go about the house putting pairs of those sticky-backed googly eyes (available in craft shops) onto small objects – like an apple in the fruit bowl, the pen pot, the salt shaker, the toilet roll holder... It'll bring the objects alive! (They peel off easily when you want to remove them.)

SAME BUT DIFFERENT:

Fairy Larder: For some girls, it may be more appealing to turn the food into a fairy's ingredients with enticing names like 'Dawn dew drops', 'Fairy dust' and 'Crushed fallen stars'!

 IF YOU LIKE THIS, YOU MIGHT LIKE...PANTS ON FIRE! P.76

Word Towers

Transform building bricks into towers of words – and give them reading practice without them even realising!

What you need:

- Plastic building bricks
- Oblong stickers
- A pen

Age: 4-6

A bit of background

Just at the age when my daughter moved on from chunky building bricks to more fiddly, nimble-fingered small building bricks, she was also starting to learn to read at school. So rather than get rid of the bricks, I decided to use them in a different way – one which would be fun for her but also give her reading practice and help her to master the lists of 'sight words' she was bringing home from school.

What I did

I got a large pack of oblong stickers that would fit on the side of the bricks. Then I wrote a different word on each sticker and stuck one on the side of each brick. Now, my daughter would be able to make sentences with the bricks by joining them together in a tower.

As well as lots of her sight words, old and new, I included my daughter and her friends' names and some silly or unusual words too – she particularly requested *meerkat* and *poo*! I did

LOTS of words (at least 150) to give lots of scope for different sentences.

I cut the stickers roughly to the size of each word and stuck the shorter words on the shortest bricks, medium-length words on medium bricks and long words on the longest bricks. You can stick words on both sides of the bricks if you want to.

To start my daughter off, I made a couple of word towers of my own to show her the idea. She began tentatively with sentences like *He is clever* and *I love chocolate* but was soon building really tall towers with long sentences. It was a big hit!

A few days later, when her friend came round to play I heard them killing themselves laughing on the living room floor as they got more and more creative making crazy sentences like *Can a monkey milk a cow?* and *You like to eat poo cake!* They were having great fun, oblivious to the educational value of what they were doing. They even started asking for stickers to write and add their own words!

TIPS: Make duplicates (four or five) of very high frequency words like *a, the, I, is* and *are*. Write verbs with an *s* at the end on one side of the brick to go with *he, she* and names e.g. *He likes sausages*, and without an s on the other side to go with *'I', 'You'* and *'They'* e.g. *I like sausages*.

AND ANOTHER IDEA...

Do you have lots of storybooks your children have grown out of? Have fun with your kids 'releasing them into the wild' for others to enjoy through http://www.bookcrossing.com. You might leave one book on a bench and another hanging from a tree! Later you can look on the website to see who the finders were!

She eats pink eggs for break- -fast every morning

 IF YOU LIKE THIS, YOU MIGHT LIKE...THE WALL OF FOAM P.104

Black-out Poems

Here's a fun and original way for your children to produce poetry – without a daunting blank piece of paper!

What you need:

- Newspapers
- Marker pens

A bit of background

This idea is inspired by American artist Austin Kleon who is famous for his 'black-out poems'. Usually when you write a poem, you put words down on paper. But Austin makes a poem by *taking* words *away* from the paper! He chooses an article in a newspaper and blacks out the words he doesn't want with a marker pen until he is left with a short poem he likes. Here is an example of the sort thing he does:

This is perfect to do with older kids. In the words of Austin himself, here's how you do it:

- Grab a newspaper.
- Grab a marker.
- Find an article.
- Cross out words, leaving behind the ones you like.
- Pretty soon you'll have a poem.

What we did

I tried it with my son when he was 13. I showed him some of Austin's poems online first to give him the concept and stimulate his creative juices! Then we dug out a couple of free local newspapers from our recycling box, flicked through them looking at the headlines and cut out a bunch of articles we thought might work well. Then with marker pen in hand, we each chose some to read closely – and got busy blacking out!

It's quite a challenge to pick out words from a functional, informative piece of writing to make 'art'! It'll make your brain creak in unusual but pleasurable ways – and it's very, very satisfying when you produce something you're pleased with!

The poems can be as short or as long as you like. You may get more than one poem from the same article. There are little tricks that can help like only using part of a word and blacking out the rest e.g. ~~work~~ing, or using words in a different way to the way they're used in the article e.g. the verb *show* could become the noun *show*.

Here are two of the poems my son 'wrote'. Both are from a newspaper article with the headline: *Spitfire mission begins take-off.*

A second
Rarely legendary
Already finished
and
Splendid manoeuvrability
Handle women the same

> **TIPS**: Local newspapers and tabloids work better than broadsheets because the stories and language tend to be simpler and more accessible for children. If they come up with any really good/inspiring/motivating/uplifting/funny poems, you could frame each one in a mini clip frame and display them as a group.

AND ANOTHER IDEA...

Homemade magnetic poetry: Children can flick through newspapers and magazines cutting out words they like. Stick each word to a piece of adhesive magnetic tape (easy to buy online) and paint with varnish or clear nail polish. Put them on the fridge and they will have their own, very personal set of magnetic poetry in a spectacular array of fonts and colours! Remember to include lots of useful words too, like 'is' and 'the'.

IF YOU LIKE THIS, YOU MIGHT LIKE...STORY DICE P.74

HIDDEN TREASURE

Two ingenious treasure hunts, one for big kids and one for little ones

- Shopkeepers' Treasure Hunt BRAVE + BOLD!
- Picture Trail Treasure Hunt

Shopkeepers' Treasure Hunt

Set your children a treasure hunt with real, live, human clues!

What you need:

- Plain cards
- Envelopes
- Treasure (bag of sweets, coins etc.)
- Willing shopkeepers!

BRAVE + BOLD!

Age: 6-13

A bit of background

I heard about a very inventive treasure hunt in a park in Lancaster where children had to find dancers hiding in different places around the park and learn a short set of dance moves from each of them. When they'd 'collected' all the moves, they joined them together into a dance routine and performed it en masse!

I loved this idea of using humans as the clues in a treasure hunt! Wouldn't it be satisfying and engaging for the kids if I could make them a treasure hunt that involved interacting with 'real people' in the 'real world'? This is what I came up with!

What we did

I used ten random shopkeepers in the small town where I live as the humans (an area or suburb of a city that your children know well would work too). Each shopkeeper was to have a clue. The solution to each clue would be the name of a shop. The children would be led from shop to shop collecting the clues from the shopkeepers. The final clue would be a simple map with an X marking the exact spot where I'd hidden the treasure. (I chose a bag of chocolate coins and hid them in a park somewhere it wouldn't be found by anyone else or eaten or weed on by a dog!).

I wrote the ten clues, put them in envelopes, marked them Clue 1, Clue 2, etc. and delivered them to the shopkeepers — explaining to them what I was up to and to expect two children asking for a clue! All of them were more than happy to take part and tucked them down the side of their till or under the counter like they had a special secret.

Later that same day, I gave my (then) 10-year old son and his friend the first clue. I felt they were old enough and it was safe enough for them do the treasure hunt on their own —

although I made sure they took a mobile phone so they could phone me if they got stuck on a clue. However, you could always accompany your children – but stay very much in the background.

The clues were a mixture of riddles, rhymes, anagrams, gap fills, cryptic messages and codes. You need to make sure they are the right level for your child – challenging but doable.

My son and his friend got high as kites on this treasure hunt. They became totally involved in the process and the prize was merely a bonus. The only downside is that my son frequently pesters me to make another one!

TIPS:
• Choose shops you know your children know the names and location of. Small, independent shops with one shopkeeper work best. If the staff are likely to change shifts, ask them if they'll tell the person who takes over from them about the treasure hunt and where the clue is!

• Don't get in a muddle when you're delivering the clues. Make sure each shopkeeper has the clue to the NEXT shop, not their own shop! It helps to work backwards from the treasure, delivering Clue 10 first.

Example Clues:

Here are some example clues to give you inspiration for making up your own clues.

Fill the gap clues

What word goes in these spaces?

He was -------- (A) his head off!

And what word goes in these spaces?

chicken ------- (B) cube

Now work this out to get the answer: The A + B = ?

[Answer: The Laughing Stock - a joke and party shop]

'It rhymes with...' clues

What shop rhymes with Poo Glider?!

[Answer: Sue Ryder]

Cryptic clues

What shop is this?

H2O + abbreviation for street + IIIIIIIII = ?

[Answer: water + st + ones = Waterstones]

Secret code clues

Look at this secret code.

□ = a   % = b $ = c   & = d   £ = e   (continue for whole alphabet)

Now work out the name of this shop: $! # £

Rhyming clues

What shop do you think this rhyme is talking about?

If you go down to the shop today
You'd better go in disguise
If you go down to the shop today
You're in for a big surprise

[Answer: The Teddy Bear Shop]

Muddled word clues

Unmuddle these words to get the name of the next shop:

Amfox kobo hops

[Answer: Oxfam Book Shop]

 IF YOU LIKE THIS, YOU MIGHT LIKE...THE DICE-THROWING WALK P.30

Picture Trail Treasure Hunt

You don't have to wait until your child can read clues to set them a treasure hunt – here's how to make one they'll love using just pictures

What you need:

- Post-its
- A pen

A bit of background

Even before my son could say the words 'treasure hunt' properly (*chesha-unt!*), let alone read them, we found a way to set him treasure hunts that had him scampering around the house like an excited rabbit!

Rather than using words, each clue was a picture. We took 10 post-its and drew an object from our house on each one e.g. the telephone, the bath, my son's toy drum kit, the washing machine, his bed, a houseplant, the fridge, his favourite toy aeroplane and the toothbrush pot.

They should be objects that are easy for you to draw. The drawings don't have to be good – but they must be recognizable! Choose objects that there are only one of in the house and from lots of different rooms. If the weather was good, we also included some objects that were in the garden (bench, ride-on tractor, peg basket...).

First we hid the 'treasure' – which might be a chocolate bar or a very small toy – on, under, behind or inside one of the objects we had drawn (e.g. inside the washing machine is a good place!). Then, working backwards from where the treasure was, we hid the other picture clues – one by one – on, under, behind or inside the other objects e.g. if the treasure was in the washing machine, the picture of the washing machine could go on his toy aeroplane, the picture of the toy aeroplane could go in the bath and so on. Don't put consecutive clues in the same room, but spread them out around the house, so that the children will have to do a bit of travelling!

When you've finished setting up, there should be one picture left over – this will be the first clue, the one you give to your child to start the treasure hunt off.

When you're ready, explain to your child how the treasure hunt works and that each clue is an object in the house. They should look at the picture, work out what the object is, go to that object and find the next clue – until they reach the treasure!

Then give them the first clue, sit back and watch them go! Try to leave them to figure things out on their own and only help if they are really, really stuck.

My son was still requesting this type of treasure hunt way beyond when he'd learned to read!

TIPS: This treasure hunt is great for Easter time. Instead of just giving Easter eggs to the children, use them as the treasure!

IF YOU LIKE THIS, YOU MIGHT LIKE...WORD TOWERS P.82

SPICING UP EVERYDAY LIFE

Add an element of surprise and fun to the day-to-day routine

- Jam Tart Tray Dinner
- The Ironing Board Hair Wash
- The Surprise Letter
- Ice-cubes in the Bath!
- The Weekend House-swap
- The Wall of Foam

Jam Tart Tray Dinner

**Dinner time becomes more fun than functional
with this special meal of compartments**

What you need:

Age: 3-12

- Jam tart tray
- Lots of different finger foods (you'll probably already
  have lots of suitable ones in your fridge and cupboard anyway)

A bit of background

To break routine once in a while, I give my children what we call a 'jam tart tray dinner' in front of the TV. It turns dinner – or lunch – into a special treat for them and (truth be told!) gives me a break from cooking when I'm feeling lazy.

What I did

I take a jam tart tray – you know, those baking sheets with twelve hollows for each jam tart or muffin. Then I raid my fridge and larder for twelve separate types of food and put one into each hollow. I use some foods that are familiar to my children to stay within their comfort zone, but also use it as an opportunity to sneak in a couple of foods they haven't tried before – to stretch their palate and encourage adventurous eating.

Kids absolutely love this style of eating. The fun factor of the meal can make even fussy eaters with very narrow tastes forget to say 'yuk' to new foods. I tell my children that they can eat as much or as little of the tray as they like and leave them to it. You might be surprised how your children get stuck in!

FOODS YOU COULD INCLUDE ARE:

cubes of cheese

carrot sticks

maltesers

sunflower seeds

baby marshmallows

crisps

twiglets

hummus

dips

cucumber slices

tofu chunks

popcorn

apple slices

raisins

chocolate buttons

cherry tomatoes

chorizo slices

cornflakes (dry)

orange segments

TIPS: This idea works really well at kids' parties as a novelty – and to keep junk food intake under control! When bowls and plates of food are put out on the table, most kids will inevitably take mountains of crisps and chocolate fingers and leave the carrot sticks and apple slices alone. But if you give each child their own individual jam tart tray already filled with a bit of both healthy and junk stuff, you can limit the damage!

I usually fill just two or three of the hollows with sweet stuff, but I don't tell them they have to eat those last 'as pudding' – that would spoil the fun. In the jam tart tray dinner, all foods are equal!

 IF YOU LIKE THIS, YOU MIGHT LIKE...ACTIVITIES ADVENT CALENDAR P.126

The Ironing-board Hair Wash

Transform the chore of a hair wash into a fun event – with the unlikely aid of an ironing board!

Age: 3-8

What you need:

- Ironing board
- Kitchen sink
- A jug
- Shampoo
- A towel

A bit of background

This idea is from my Nanny Joyce, my maternal grandmother, who had a mischievous twinkle in her eye and was always on the lookout for ways to put a bit of quirky fun into everyday life. She saw the 1970s power cuts as an opportunity to make toast with us by the gas fire. She spontaneously took us swimming in the dark at an outdoor pool in her friend's garden – when we thought we were going to bed.

And every so often she would announce out of the blue, in the daytime, 'Who'd like to have their hair washed on the ironing board?' For some reason, at age 5, 6 or even 8, this made a hair wash the most exciting thing in the world. The ironing board would come out of the cupboard, creak open and we'd clamber on one by one. We'd lie back and giggle, enjoying each massage of the head and the scent of the shampoo like we never did in the bath.

What you do

This is great for little ones who hate having their hair washed. Miraculously, something that is usually a traumatic, tearful affair becomes something they love, enjoy and relax into.

An ironing board, it turns out, is exactly the right height for a kitchen sink and lying back on it means your child doesn't get any water or shampoo in their eyes. Just put the square end of the ironing board at the sink and fold up a towel to make a comfy pillow to bridge the edge of the ironing board and the edge of the sink. Use a jug to pour the water.

Oh, and just for laughs, don't forget to ask hairdressery type questions like, 'Is that the right temperature for you madam?' and 'Going anywhere nice on your holidays?'

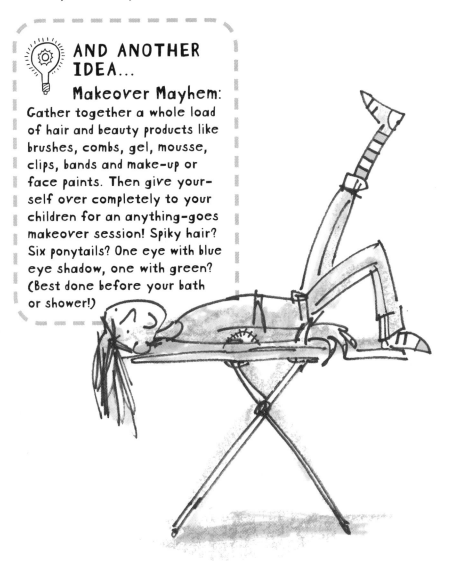

AND ANOTHER IDEA...

Makeover Mayhem: Gather together a whole load of hair and beauty products like brushes, combs, gel, mousse, clips, bands and make-up or face paints. Then give yourself over completely to your children for an anything-goes makeover session! Spiky hair? Six ponytails? One eye with blue eye shadow, one with green? (Best done before your bath or shower!)

 IF YOU LIKE THIS, YOU MIGHT LIKE...LICKETY WALLPAPER P.12

The Surprise Letter

Surprise your child with a personal letter from you to them – delivered by the postman

What you need:

- Paper
- Pen
- Envelope
- Stamp

Age: 3-12

A bit of background

My son always rushes to the front door when he hears the post. 'I'll get it, I'll get it,' he shouts, as if he's expecting delivery of an ipad-X-Box-Playstation-Wii-extraordinaire! He's always disappointed: A gas bill, a bank statement, some junk mail... I'm not sure what he's hoping for. Post has only ever come for him on his birthday – unless you count the time he got a letter addressed to him reminding us that he was due for an eye test.

What I did

So...I decided to make the thud of the letters on the doormat a little less boring for him one day! I simply wrote him a letter, put our address on it, stuck a stamp on it and posted it in a post box.

It's a great way to surprise and amuse your child and make them feel special. What kind of thing can you write in your letter? Anything you like: What

you like about them, how you've noticed them change recently, plans and ideas of things you want to do with them, jokes, doodles...

I sneakily watched my son open his letter through the hatch between our kitchen and living room and saw him grin and blush with a mixture of pleasure and embarrassment!

If you're lucky (don't hold your breath), they'll write you a letter back!

 AND ANOTHER IDEA... A Parent-child Notebook: Take a blank notebook and write a message to your child on the first page. Leave it in their bedroom for them to write a message back to you. Keep passing it backwards and forwards.

DID YOU KNOW...?

Research shows that humans are more likely to believe and remember what they read than what they hear. Expressing your love in writing to your child is more powerful than saying it!

 IF YOU LIKE THIS, YOU MIGHT LIKE...THE WEEKEND HOUSE-SWAP P.102

Ice-cubes in the Bath!

Forget rubber ducks! Make bath time extra fun by adding some unusual ice-cubes

What you need:

- Ice-cube trays and/or muffin tray
- Food colourings
- Tiny toys and objects

Age: 3-7

A bit of background

When my daughter was 3-years-old she had a fascination with ice. Whenever we went to a restaurant or pub and there was ice in our drinks, she insisted on us fishing it clumsily out of our drinks for her. She loved crunching it between her teeth, but she also loved holding it in her hands, watching it melt – not altogether practical or polite in a restaurant!

What you do

The bath is the perfect place to play with ice-cubes! No puddles, no mess. Better still, you can make ice-cubes at home which are even more appealing to young children. By simply adding several drops of food colouring to the water in each compartment of the ice-cube tray – red in some, green in others, and so on – you can create a colourful collection of rainbow ice-cubes.

Another idea is to make bigger ice-cubes using a muffin tray with deep hollows and 'hide' a small toy or object in each one: A tiny plastic toy animal, a penny, a doll's shoe, a button... Your child will see the object magically captured inside the ice to be fully revealed and released once it has melted. For the double-whammy add food colouring to these ones too.

This idea only takes a few minutes for you to prepare, but up to half an hour of fun for them. It's especially good for making sleepover baths with friends or cousins extra special.

Just fill your bath with water, get your child to climb in and then start adding the cubes! And just in case you're wondering, unless you add loads, the ice-cubes won't make the bath water cold!

 BEWARE! Of course, keep a beady eye on very young children with small objects they might put in their mouths!

AND ANOTHER
IDEA...

Spaghetti Pool:

Add some cooked spaghetti to their paddling pool water in the summer for some squelchy, squidgy fun! You could throw in some tongs, colanders and spaghetti servers too. Tell them not to eat it though!

 IF YOU LIKE THIS, YOU MIGHT LIKE...IT'S A MUD, MUD WORLD! P.112

The Weekend House-swap

Give your children a taste of other children's lives – and a very cheap weekend away

What you need:

- Nothing (except toothbrushes, pyjamas, etc.)

A bit of background

I've always fancied one of those house-swap holidays. You know, where I get to stay in a 5-bedroom (all ensuite) house with heated swimming pool in Florida and they get to stay in my 2 ½-bed house in England with dodgy bathroom shower and wobbly garden bench! I'll get round to organizing it one day,

but meanwhile I took the idea, shrunk it and suggested it to British friends and family (who have children): Were any of them interested in a mini house-swap – just for the weekend? We found friends in Bristol and family in Norwich who were both up for it – nice cheap city breaks for us and a dose of country (ish) living for them.

Imagine what fun and how relaxed it is to go and stay in someone else's house when they're not there! Free accommodation in a house already 'broken in' by children – toys, books, stain on the rug?! You don't have to make an effort to be good guests and there are no tricky situations – you know, like when you usually eat dinner at 5 and they eat at 7 and your kids are starving!

Apart from being able to explore the area at our own pace, to our own agenda, our children loved living in the shoes of other children: Discovering their toys, choosing from their DVDS, feeding their guinea pigs, having a bath with their bubble bath, choosing a bedtime story from their bookshelf, sleeping in their beds (bunk beds – we don't have them at home) and eating their cereal in the morning (Chocolate Ready Brek no less!).

Even the physical details of the houses were a source of amusement. A lot of time was spent going up and down the ladder to the new loft conversion in Norwich and – even more exciting – going through the secret bookcase into a hidden room in the basement in Bristol!

If you arrange to 'swap' babysitters too like we did, you can have a grown-up night out in the new place!

AND ANOTHER IDEA...

Truck Stop: When you're travelling by car with kids, avoid the queues and high prices of service stations and stop at a transport cafe instead. Anyone can use them and they're quiet, cheap and clean. Transport-mad boys will love entering 'lorry driver world' with all the artics parked outside! http://www.transportcafe.co.uk/ will tell you where there's one on your route.

TIP: To add authenticity and fun to your mini-holiday, get the children to make a welcome pack for the children who are coming to stay at their house. It could have information and drawings about their favourite places to visit locally, how much food to feed the fish, where the sweets are kept, names of teddy bears...

 IF YOU LIKE THIS, YOU MIGHT LIKE...GRAPH OF THE DAY P.72

IF YOU LIKE THIS, YOU MIGHT LIKE...GRAPH OF THE DAY P.72

The Wall of Foam

Turn your bathroom tiles into a huge art canvas – with a simple pack of craft foam

Age: 3–8

What you need:

- Craft foam

A bit of background

We have a couple of sets of those chubby foam pieces that children can stick to the tiles at bath time – one of cars and roads and one of girls and clothes. The problem with these, though is that they are too thick to stick really well and the ways you can arrange them are rather limited and uninspiring.

The solution? Make your own pieces with craft foam – the stuff that comes in sheets of assorted colours which you can buy very cheaply in art and craft shops or even pound shops.

It's thin so it sticks really, really well and there is absolutely no limit to the patterns, pictures and designs

children can make with it on the bathroom wall.

What I did

I got one packet and cut the sheets into shapes of different sizes, such as squares, triangles, rectangles, circles, hearts and strips. I made lots and lots – about a 100 pieces – to give infinite creative possibilities. Then I dipped them in water and stuck them randomly on the tiles next to the bath ready for action.

When I put my (then 4-year-old) daughter in the bath that night she was delighted to discover them and immediately set to work making geometric patterns, then faces, then rows of houses and then mazes. It was tricky getting her out of the bath that night!

The funny thing was that when I sent my 11-year old son in to have a shower later than evening, he came out afterwards and said, 'What's that stuff in the bathroom? It's cool. I was designing flags and football emblems with it!'

The creations left behind on the wall day in, day out, actually look rather good and make the bathroom a lot more cheerful and interesting!

One day, I even found my daughter and her friend standing in the empty bath, fully clothed, making pictures together!

TIP: Give your children some children's scissors when they're in the bath and let them cut out shapes of their own to their exact requirements!

AND ANOTHER IDEA...
The Candle-lit Bath: Candle-lit baths aren't just for grown-ups. Surprise your children when you call them for their bath with a dark bathroom lit only by candles! Of course, make sure the candles are completely out of their reach, or better still, use flameless LED candles.

IF YOU LIKE THIS, YOU MIGHT LIKE...DIY MARBLE RUN P.56

GARDEN ANTICS

**Imaginative ideas to keep
them entertained and happy
in your own back garden**

- The Music Tree
- The Mini-market Stall Holder
- It's a Mud, Mud World!
- The Unscary Scarecrow

The Music Tree

Turn a tree (or washing line) into a place where your children can entertain themselves making music!

Age: 3-6

What you need:

- A tree (or washing line)
- A variety of metal objects such as kitchen utensils, saucepans
- Wind chimes
- Wooden spoons

A bit of background

Our neighbours have a metal wind chime hanging from a tree in their garden. Sometimes as I'm falling asleep, I hear it tinkling gently in the breeze. But one night instead of soothing me, it set my brain whizzing...

What about hanging lots of makeshift instruments from the branches of the tree in our garden and turning it into the magic 'music tree'? I could give my (then 3-year-old) daughter and her friends some wooden spoons to hit them with and they could enjoy making sweet music!

First, I needed to find some suitable objects that would make different sounds. A scavenge of the local charity and pound shops and one car boot sale got me: A metal wind chime (which I dismantled into its separate pieces), two saucepans and two saucepan lids, a metal bowl, a metal sieve, a metal cheese grater and even an old tambourine. I only chose things which had handles or holes that I'd be able use to hang them onto the tree with. I also got several wooden spoons.

We only have one small tree in our garden – a gnarled, twisty, unidentified thing (though quite attractive in its own way!) but if you don't have a tree, a washing line would be fine. I tied each object to different parts of the tree securely, with strong string so that they all hung at slightly different heights but so that they could all be reached easily enough by a young child. I spaced them out so that they were far enough apart not to bang into each other when they were hit, but close enough for the children to be able to move between them niftily. The tree looked pretty quirky! I grabbed a wooden spoon and gave it a test run. It was rather satisfying and surprising how many different sounds and tones you could make!

The music tree was a roaring – and loud – success! When the girls saw the tree, they ran to it like squirrels being chased! After lots of initial experimentation, I found them singing and bashing a tuneless rendition of *The Grand Old Duke of York*! My favourite time though was when I caught my daughter on her own, singing *If you're happy and you know it*, hit the pan (bash, bash), inventing different lines to complete each verse!

I guess you could call it music therapy.

TIP: At the risk of people thinking you're very odd, take a wooden spoon to the shops or car boot sale so you can test out what noise things make before you buy them!

AND ANOTHER IDEA...

The Non-sand Sandpit: Make their sandpit exciting again by filling it with rice instead of sand! You can buy a huge sack of it in Asian supermarkets. Rice slips through sand toys easily and feels and sounds really satisfying!

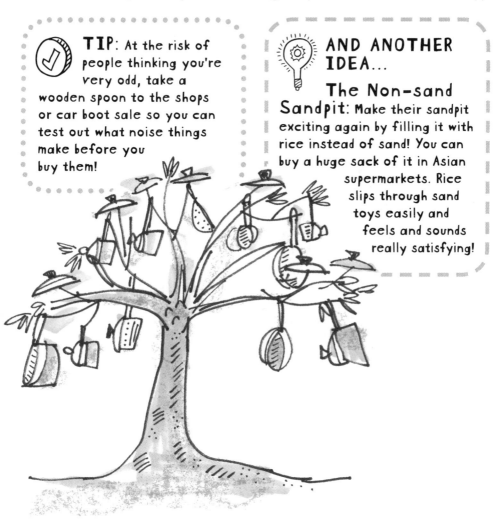

IF YOU LIKE THIS, YOU MIGHT LIKE...ICE-CUBES IN THE BATH P.100

The Mini-market Stall Holder

Age: 3-6

Manning a makeshift market stall outside your house can keep children happy all day!

What you need:

- Home made cakes
- Portable table
- Tablecloth
- Paper/card to make a sign and price labels
- Pens
- Toy till or money belt
- Small change

A bit of background

Children love to play 'shops' when they're little. I can't tell you how many tedious hours I've spent at my living room coffee table pretend-buying toy cars/teddy bears/drawings/old chocolate buttons from my son or daughter. So think how they will jump at the chance to be in charge of a real stall with real merchandise and real money!

What we did

One sunny Saturday morning when my son was 6, we spent a bit of time knocking up some small cakes like jam tarts and chocolate crispie cakes. I helped him set up his stall in the front garden with a table, tablecloth and his toy till with some spare change in it. He also wanted to wear a money belt for that market trader look! I got him to make a sign for his stall (Freddie's cake stall) and price labels for the cakes. We discussed reasonable prices and any special offers (1 for 10p, 4 for 30p?).

Once I'd made sure he knew how to tout his products politely and confidently to neighbours and other passers-by (something like 'Would you like to buy some cakes?'), I left him to it, keeping a sneaky eye on proceedings in the background (i.e. I sat in my living room with a book facing out the window!).

Astonishingly, he manned his stall for five solid hours. He enjoyed it so much he even insisted on having his 'lunch break' on the job! He practised his mental arithmetic, presentation, marketing and people skills all in one go and at the end of the day, he'd made £9 (though this was mainly because most people thought his prices were too low and gave him more!).

The customers were happy too. As one woman who pulled up in her car said, 'Snacks for all the family for only 30p!'

TIPS: Choose a weekend day to do this when there are more people out and about.

• Make cakes which are quick and easy – this idea is about selling, not cooking!

SAME BUT DIFFERENT:

Toy stall: Let them set up a stall to sell the toys and books they have grown out of. It's a good chance to de-clutter and maybe even make some money for charity.

 IF YOU LIKE THIS, YOU MIGHT LIKE...COMMUNAL ART P.40

It's a Mud, Mud World!

Mud – dirty, sticky, messy. You can try to keep your children away from it... or let them get stuck in and enjoy it in imaginative ways!

Age: 3-8

What you need:

- A small, soily area of your garden
- For mini construction site: toy trucks, diggers and other construction toys, planks of wood (optional), plastic guttering (optional)
- For chocolate cup cakes: paper cake cases, spoons, flowers, leaves, stones

A bit of background

At a farm museum near us, there is a wonderful 'mud pie kitchen' for children to play with. It definitely divides parents into two distinct groups: There's the keep-away-from-there-you'll-get-filthy types and the sit-back-and-relax-I'll-deal-with-the-dirt-later gang. Almost every single child, however, is attracted to it like a wasp to jam! Sitting watching a gaggle of them enjoying it so much, I thought about ways kids could indulge in a bit of fun and sloppy mud play in their own back garden.

What to do

The mini building site

This will appeal to boys more than girls, generally speaking. Choose a spot of your garden which you don't mind giving over to the children, like a section of a flowerbed. Now turn it into a mini building site by digging it over to loosen the soil and landscaping it a little with some mounds and dips to make it more interesting. You may need to add a bit of water to moisten it. Then bring out all their toy trucks, diggers, bulldozers, cranes and other construction vehicles and leave them to it. The tyres of trucks can mark out tracks, diggers can scoop up soil, cranes can lift rocks and twigs.... and whatever else their imagination comes up with! You could even add some planks of wood to make ramps and pieces of plastic guttering to make chutes for the vehicles.

Chocolate cup cakes

Now for a more refined way to play with mud if there is such a thing: Old-fashioned mud pie making gone up market! Again, you will need to dig over a small area of soil and add a little water. Give your children some small paper cake cases and set them the challenge of creating the most realistic 'chocolate cup cakes' they can! They can use a spoon to fill the paper cases with mud and push it down, and then smooth off the tops with the back of the spoon. Next, they can get artistic, decorating the tops with flower petals, tiny leaves, pretty pebbles and bits of twig. If they leave them in the sunshine to 'bake' and then present them nicely on a plate, they can look surprisingly chocolatey and authentic! Your kids might think it's even more fun to bake them in the oven (250°C/Gas mark 9 for 15 minutes). My daughter got a lot of fun out of offering her cakes and trying to trick people!

Finally, chuck kids in bath and scrub well!

AND ANOTHER IDEA...
The Incredible Train Journey: A wooden toy train set becomes 'fresh' and exciting again if you bring it outside into the garden. Let your children set it up so it winds around trees, through bushes, between plant pots...

 IF YOU LIKE THIS, YOU MIGHT LIKE...IT'S GONE ALL MOULDY P.16

The Unscary Scarecrow

Make a quirky scarecrow to liven up your garden and put a smile on the faces of passers-by

Age: 3–13

What you need:

- Two pieces of wood (e.g. broom handle, straight branch)
- Big pack of straw
- Old pillowcase
- Old clothes including gloves and accessories

A bit of background

Whilst driving down country lanes in Shropshire, we kept spotting scarecrows positioned in unlikely places by the side of the road: One dressed as a policeman, one leaning against a postbox... They weren't meant to scare birds away, they were simply to amuse.

What we did

I thought why don't we put a friendly scarecrow in our garden somewhere? We don't grow a single vegetable or fruit, but it'd be fun for the children to make – and add a bit of humour to the neighbourhood.

First we went scarecrow clothes shopping! We decided it would be more interesting to avoid the traditional Worzel Gummidge look. So rooting through the local charity shops, there were lots of serious discussions to be had and important decisions to be made, like: Pink beret or hippy bandana? Stripy jumper or high visibility waistcoat? And would an old lady's handbag create the right look?... Finally, we popped into the pet shop for a giant pack of straw to stuff the scarecrow with.

Back at home we looked around for things we could use to make a cross frame and found an old broom handle (for the vertical 'body') and a straight branch which was a bit shorter (for the horizontal 'arms'). We tied them together tightly with strong string and dressed them with the clothes we'd bought. We added an old plain pillowcase for the head and gardening gloves for the hands. Next we stuffed it all tightly with straw, tying the neck, waist, wrists and ankles with string to keep it in. We used a permanent marker to draw on his face and gave him hair by gluing pieces of straw to the inside of the hat. Then just a few final touches (flower in his buttonhole, sunglasses…) and he was ready to be hammered into position.

So Eric (as we called him) stood in our garden for many months, smiling at passers-by over the garden wall. He wasn't the most attractive of scarecrows. His head was a little on the large side and he had short, fat legs, but he was a very likeable chap!

When the wind and rain had finally got the better of him, we laid him to rest. 'Let's make another one,' said my daughter. 'A lady this time. We could sit her on the bench in the front garden.'

 IF YOU LIKE THIS, YOU MIGHT LIKE…THE WITCH'S LARDER P.80

'TIS THE SEASON TO BE...

Fresh inspiration to help celebrate those special days of the year

- Shrunken Heads
- Secret Christmas Mission BRAVE + BOLD!
- The New Year's Interview
- Reverse Trick or Treating
- Activities Advent Calendar

Shrunken Heads

At Halloween, carving pumpkins is the norm – but apples can be much, much scarier!

What you need:

- Large apples
- Bowl of water
- Two lemons
- Salt
- Peelers or small knives,
- Toothpicks
- Grains of rice
- Cloves or peppercorns (optional)
- Strands of hair from a Halloween wig (optional)

Age: 3 to grown-up

A bit of background

Both my kids are fascinated by the grotesque shrunken heads at the Pitt Rivers Museum in Oxford: Heads of Amazonian tribes people which have been severed, skinned, de-skulled and boiled by their enemies until they were tiny and distorted and ready to be used as trophies!

I thought it would be fun for the children to make some shrunken heads of their own to display at Halloween – but using apples rather than humans! The process is a lot simpler, but the results are extremely effective and – believe me – just as sinister.

What you do

You'll need to start roughly two weeks before Halloween. Take some apples – the bigger the better as you're going to shrink them – and peel them. Two apples per person would be enough, but you can each make as many as you like.

Now get creative! Carve a face into each apple using the end of a peeler or a small knife. Make eye sockets, eyebrows, a nose, a mouth and even ears if you can. A toothpick can be useful too to eek out bits of flesh and create lines for wrinkles. The bigger and more exaggerated the features the better because small details will be lost in the shriveling process. So you want deep-set eyes, prominent eyebrow ridges and large noses. Try different types of faces on different apples. Don't worry if you make little mistakes here and there because these won't show when the apples are shriveled!

Now you can add some grisly finishing touches. Push individual grains of rice into the mouth at angles to make jagged, crooked teeth. Leave lots of gaps – if you just place one or two teeth at the top and a few at the bottom, the effect will be much more hideous! If you like, you can also push cloves or peppercorns into the centre of the eyes, but empty eye sockets are also good for that sunken-eyed effect.

Finally, soak the apples for 10 minutes in a small bowl of water with two tablespoons of salt and the juice of two lemons mixed thoroughly into it. This will stop the apples rotting and going too brown.

All you have to do now is leave your apples somewhere warm and dry (an airing cupboard is ideal) for two weeks to metamorphosize! As they dry out, they will slowly shrink and shrivel until the faces are unrecognizable and truly gruesome. If you have a Halloween wig, you could glue a few strands of hair to the top!

At Halloween, put them in your window to impress Trick or Treaters and keep the enemy away!

TIPS: If you forget or don't have time to carve your apples in advance of Halloween, you can cheat and do them at the last minute – put them in the oven for 3-6 hours at 190/Gas Mark 5 instead! The results are almost as effective.

IF YOU LIKE THIS, YOU MIGHT LIKE...IT'S GONE ALL MOULDY P.16

Secret Christmas Mission!

Use a little bit of sneakiness to surprise friends and spread the festive spirit

Age: 6 to grown-up

What you need:

- Decorations with a Christmas message
- Strong waterproof tape

A bit of background

Imagine this: You wake up on Christmas morning, throw back the curtains and there on the windowsill outside is a robin with a twig in its beak holding a little banner saying, 'Merry Christmas!' in sparkly gold writing. Wouldn't that add to your glowy, warm, magical Christmassy feeling? And wouldn't it create a sense of mystery: Who could have put that there? And when did they do it?

Well, it might have been my son and me!

What we did

Last freezing cold Christmas Eve, me and my then 12-year-old son put on our very warmest coats and snuck around our town to (six) friends' houses with some artificial (but very realistic) robins we'd bought in the Christmas section of the pound shop. We'd written 'Merry Christmas' banners with a gold pen on red card and glued them onto twigs which we'd then glued to the robins' beaks.

At each house, we snuck up to the windowsill to carefully position a robin there with strong tape so that it was peeping in the window.

It felt exciting, whispering and walking on tiptoes so as not to get caught – particularly tricky if people hadn't drawn their curtains yet! My son said he felt like a burglar – but a burglar who gives rather than takes!

Festive season over, we started to get some feedback. 'I was just washing up the breakfast stuff and the kids were all excited, shouting, "Look! Look!" and pointing to the window. It was so funny,' said one friend. Another said, 'It was so lovely. It made my day. In fact, we loved it so much, we're going to do something similar next year!'

Of course, it's up to you whether you tell them it was you who did it or not. We couldn't resist!

TIPS: Only visit friends' houses and make sure they will be at home and not away on Christmas morning! (You could just do your neighbours' houses if you don't want to go too far afield.)

SAME BUT DIFFERENT:

Go your own way: You can use any decoration you like. A Christmas fairy? An elf? A toy model penguin? Or how about a big bauble with a message on it hanging in a tree?

 IF YOU LIKE THIS, YOU MIGHT LIKE...HANSEL AND GRETEL WALK P.32

The New Year's Interview

Begin each year with a series of questions to 'capture' your child at that age – and see how they change

What you need:

- A set of questions for each child
- A pen and paper

A bit of background

One New Year's Day, on a walk in the woods, we explained to my son (then 4) – best we could – what a New Year's resolution was. When it seemed he'd grasped the idea, we asked him what his resolutions were for that year. He thought very carefully and replied, 'Watch more videos.'!

Maybe New Year's resolutions work best with adults I decided! However, a New Year's *interview* works really well with children. They enjoy it and it 'freeze-frames' the things they like and think about at that particular age.

Prepare a sheet of questions. You could, for example, ask:

- What's your favourite meal? Drink? Toy? Book? TV programme? School subject? Thing to do in your free time? Place to go at the weekend?

- Tell me 3 things you *don't* like.
- Who is/are your best friend/s? (It's amazing how you forget who their friends were.)
- Say something you like and something you find annoying about each member of your family.
- What job would you like to do when you grow up?

122

- What were the best things that happened to you this past year?
- What would you like to happen this coming year?

Write the year at the top and fire away. Do it on New Year's day (if hangovers allow!) or as near to the beginning of the year as you can. Then put it somewhere safely. If you do an interview at the start of every year with the same questions, you'll have a record of how your children changed as they grew up. Even from one year to the next, there can be big differences and it can be fun to look back at the answers to last year's interview when you're doing that year's.

It may seem trivial now, but it will probably be precious to me to remember that when my daughter was 3, for example, she said what she most wanted to do in the coming year was 'Go to the moon in an aeroplane.'

 TIPS: Hold a toy or real microphone when you ask them the questions for that authentic interview feel!

 SAME BUT DIFFERENT:

Record it: You could film their answers instead. You and your kids will love watching this when they're all grown-up – and you'll see if any of their answers still hold true and if they've achieved any of their dreams!

 AND ANOTHER IDEA...

Stairway Art Gallery: As your children grow up, choose and frame some of their best drawings and paintings from each age and display them on the wall going up the stairs chronologically – toddler drawings at the bottom slowly evolving into more accomplished pieces as they grow up.

 IF YOU LIKE THIS, YOU MIGHT LIKE...GRAPH OF THE DAY P.72

Reverse Trick or Treating

Do you dread taking your children trick or treating? Turn it around and make it about giving instead of getting!

What you need:

- Halloween costumes
- Treats such as sweets or home made cakes

A bit of background

Last day of October – Halloween! The kids are all excited about that American tradition the UK has embraced of trick or treating. I scurry around for costumes, face paint and fake blood and reluctantly traipse around our neighbourhood with the children as they knock on doors. I insist we only go to the houses of people we know, but still, I hang back by gates and lampposts awkwardly. It feels intrusive and wrong. My kids are basically asking people to give them something – or else!

They both end up with plastic bags bulging with lollipops, sweets and chocolate and we go through the obligatory routine of sugar-fest–sugar rush–downer–bed. There must be a better way.

There is! Reverse the trick or treating. The kids can still have the excitement of dressing up, going out in the dark, knocking on doors... The difference?

They *give* a treat to the person whose door they've knocked on: A chocolate, a sweet, a lollipop, or – if you like baking – how about a piece of pumpkin pie?

The children knock on the door, say '*Reverse* trick or treat...we'd like to give YOU something to eat! Please take one,' and offer a plate or tray of treats. The person will be surprised, pleased, and your kids will (hopefully!) feel the pleasure of giving.

You can also decide how many sweets/lollipops you want to give your children as a treat later! Maybe we can make this the new tradition in the UK?

IF YOU LIKE THIS, YOU MIGHT LIKE…RUSSIAN DOLL ROULETTE P.46

Activities Advent Calendar

Make the countdown to Christmas extra fun and family-orientated with an alternative type of advent calendar

Age: 4–13

What you need:

- Envelopes or socks
- Tinsel
- Pegs
- Paper and pen

A bit of background

Most advent calendars in the shops seem to be pretty tacky these days. Shouldn't the countdown to Christmas be a little more magical and satisfying than a cartoon character and 24 mouthfuls of cheap chocolate?

One Christmas, I decided to substitute chocolate with things we could do. I sat down and thought of 24 activities, one for each day between 1st December and Christmas Eve. It sounds ambitious (both to think of and do!) but you can include any special trips you'd planned to do anyway (like going to see a pantomime) and you can sneak in Christmassy chores too (even putting up the Christmas tree)!

Here are some ideas:

- Watch a Christmassy film together
- Have a luxury hot chocolate – squirty cream, mini marshmallows, sprinkles…
- Go for a walk or drive to see a street where the residents have gone overboard on decorating their houses!
- Cut out paper snowflakes
- Read a Christmas bedtime story
- Have dinner by candlelight
- Make mince pies
- Go to an outdoor ice-rink
- Deliver Christmas cards in the dark by torchlight
- Learn some Christmas jokes from the Internet
- De-clutter bedrooms of unwanted toys ready for new toys!
- Visit a Santa's grotto
- Make paper chains
- Go carol singing
- Learn the names of all Santa's reindeer from the Internet

I wrote each activity on a piece of paper and put it in an envelope. Then I numbered the envelopes 1 to 24 and strung them up over the fireplace on tinsel with pegs. I used red and green mini envelopes and gold pegs to make it look Christmassy. You could peg up 12 pairs of children's or baby's Christmas themed socks instead that you could use again and again every year. There are of course also ready-made fabric advent calendars with pockets you can buy that'll last forever. It could, after all, become a new family tradition!

AND ANOTHER IDEA...

To make Christmas morning *even more* exciting for children (if that's possible!) before you go to bed on Christmas eve, tape Christmas wrapping paper over the door frame of the living room to block the way in. The children have to jump through the paper to enter the room and get to their presents!

TIPS:

• Be realistic and make sure there are plenty of easy, simple activities that you'll feel like doing even if you're exhausted!

• You can shuffle or change the activities as the days go by if you make new plans (say, halfway through you book a pantomime for the 23rd December.) Your children won't know!

 IF YOU LIKE THIS, YOU MIGHT LIKE...THE SURPRISE LETTER P.98